Contents

Dedication
Acknowledgments
Introduction

Dedication

To the many people and places close to my heart that I have mentioned in my book, if you are passed, then may God love and keep you. For those who are still here, I hope you enjoy my memories and the ones of you. Love Kev.

Acknowledgments

—∞—

As you will see from this book, many people have touched my heart and played a big part in my life.

My late mother, father and and let's not forget Eric and Jack. These people I loved with every bit of love I possessed, and they loved me in return. But without my daughters, Sharn and Hannah, life would be a world that holds no place for me. Love you both so much - Dad XX

There's still one light that burns brighter than all the above - my wife Paula. Without her love and guidance throughout our forty years of marriage and cuddling up on her mother's settee late at night, I wouldn't be the man I am today. She saved my sanity, dignity and every piece of respect I had for anyone that had touched my life. Paula, from the bottom of my heart please accept my love and gratitude, now and forever.

Love you
Big Kev xxxx

Introduction

Life was simple, times were hard, but there was plenty of love and respect in the hard-working West Yorkshire community where Kevin Graham grew up in the 1960s. There were plenty of scrapes and narrow shaves too, and brushes with authority and the law were a regular feature of his youthful days – he soon learned the unwritten rule that you never stole from, cheated or abused other people living on the Lump, the area of 300 or so houses which was home to the local community.

One of the many schemes Kevin and his mates got into to earn a few shillings was 'borrowing' chickens in order to sell their eggs – unfortunately the chickens knew their way home and their little scheme was soon uncovered. Then there was chopping sticks for firewood in return for a promised piglet, which never materialised and had probably never existed. And then there was the day when Kevin and a mate were instructed to make sausages for the local butcher and a sparrow flew into the grinder. The customers never complained.

Life wasn't quite so much fun after Kevin found that his mother had been having an affair and his father was leaving home, taking Kevin with him. Work became tougher too when he started working down the pit, and worse than tough when he decided to join the prison service. He discovered that his own sense of honesty, humanity and fair play was not shared by some of his colleagues, and the resulting fallout led to his being persecuted by senior officers and forced to leave the service, a traumatic experience which left a deep scar.

CHAPTER 1

Origins

I was born into a family which consisted of mum, dad, two brothers and one sister. They had struggled big time before my arrival, and over the next thirteen years the stress and struggle, and various tragedies and disasters, were to put a great deal of pressure on the entire family, myself included.

My mother and father were from very different backgrounds. My father was originally from a sleepy North Yorkshire village called Burton Leonard. It was a beautiful country village, and still is. He lived in a small cottage with his mother, stepfather and stepsister Mary, and they had an idyllic lifestyle. His stepfather, James Wilcox, was the local blacksmith, his lovely mother Annie was a housewife and Mary kept all the family on their toes.

My father joined the British Army at the age of 18 years in 1938, just before war broke out in Germany in 1939. He was posted to North Africa to fight with the Desert Rats against Field Marshall Rommel and the powerful German Army. Lots of brave men were killed during the following weeks, and my father was captured, along with hundreds more. The German Army force-marched them through Africa to Greece. They stopped on the island of Kos, where they were kept in a old castle with cells built in. Later they were marched to Germany. Once they arrived there, they were placed in POW camps. My father was made to work in a brickyard and told he was to rebuild the Fatherland.

He hated this work and this order. After months of work, he decided to try to escape. However this didn't work out; as he tried to leave the camp under the cover of darkness, he was spotted by border guards, who shouted, 'Halt, halt!' He carried on running, but seconds later he was shot in the knee and fell.

The guards retrieved him from the perimeter and took him to the hospital. Once he had been repaired and bandaged up, he was sent to a POW hospital.

By 1944, Germany was being forced to retreat all over Europe. It was only a matter of time before my father and his mates would be free.

After about three months in that camp, my father woke up one morning to find that there were no guards in the room. There were no guards outside, either. The prisoners just looked at one another, wondering what had happened to the Germans.

Then they heard the sound of diesel engines, getting louder and louder. All the men were praying that the engines and tanks to belong to the Americans. No one wanted to face the Russian Army. They were in luck. My father said that when he spotted the Stars and Stripes flying from one of the tanks, he broke down in tears.

Once the Americans liberated the camp they fed them and gave them chocolate. Father said, 'I thought I was in the presence of angels!'

When my father was repatriated to the UK he found himself in a hospital in Wakefield called Pinderfields. As he became more mobile he started to venture into the town and discovered the Dog and Gun public house. Working behind the bar was a young woman called Eileen White. The chemistry between them was amazing, according to my father. The relationship started to blossom and my mother introduced my father to my grandparents, Wilfred and Lucy White.

Shortly after meeting my grandparents, my father moved in with them. After just six months of being together, they were forced to marry. The term for that type of wedding was 'shotgun wedding', because it was said that if you didn't marry the girl you had managed to get pregnant, her father would hunt you down with a shotgun. Mother was pregnant with my big sister, Christine.

In December 1947 my sister arrived, and so did the snow; it was the worst winter on record, in more ways than one for Mam & Dad. They were living in a cramped pit house on the Lump, the name given to our part of the town. At the same time there were two of my mother's brothers living in the house, Lionel and Gilbert, then Gran and Grandad. So you will probably understand why I call it cramped. Over the next two years two more siblings arrived, Melvin and Trevor. That little house was beginning to seem very small.

My mother was offered a council house on Walton View. I bet she jumped at that offer. Anyway she and my dad took the house and moved down to Crofton, but she never settled in that house. She hated the fact that it had a coal cellar, because she constantly thought a burglar would use it to rob the house, although there was nothing in it but kids.

She badgered my father regularly to move, and eventually they moved to a house at 20 Oak Street, New Crofton, and that was where I came along. The day I was born, May 4 1959, was a happy day for my mother and sister. Dad probably gave me the one and only kiss he ever gave me in my hard struggle of life. Melvin came into the bedroom to see me, but only under duress. Trevor refused to look at me or even enter the room. For nine years he had been the baby of the family, and that all changed with my arrival, and I believe he never got his head around that fact. That's why for the next seventeen years he never accepted me and was constantly unpleasant to me.

To some extent I understand his concerns, because life was hard enough for young kids without having your position within the family snatched away from you. So yes I do have some sympathy, but he carried his dislike for his little brother for far too long.

I was clearly a mistake, having been born to a mining family that was already struggling. This could only spell one thing – rejection.

Growing up was hard, with two brothers hitting me and enjoying it. They would encourage me to play and at times make me feel part of the family, but the truth was never far away. This play fighting was just another way of getting retribution for my birth.

Above is a picture of my first school. I always remember my coat peg – a bloody pink elephant. Now who the hell would give a young rough and ready lad a pink elephant coat peg, in the early 60s? That's how much attention the teachers paid to the young kids who attended their school. On the first day, my mother walked me to the infants' school. The journey was approximately half a mile, and I was four years of age. As for being accompanied by mother on the second day, that never happened. For the next twelve years it was down to me to navigate myself to school. Older girls would hold your hand and make sure you were ok.

So I'm always grateful to those girls who helped me day on day during the early years. Two that I will always remember are Shirley Morris and Judy Blackledge. These two were like school angels who would oversee younger kids and make sure we arrived at school safe.

School was something the Government insisted we attend throughout my twelve years within the education system. Teachers were happy if you displayed numerical and literary skills. After that, they knew we were all bound for working-class jobs. But in those days all the industries were owned by the government, so there were thousands of vacancies that needed filling. And you guessed right – we were the fillers.

Life for youths in the 70s was a different world from the one the youth of today experience. I didn't know a single person in the 70s who went off to university. Today the young people who achieve within the education system are rewarded with a place in a university, and rightly so.

One of my best friends throughout those precious learning years was Steven Tottey. His parents, Wally and Bessie, were called to our junior school, where the Headmaster, Mr Oswald, told them that Steven was the most intelligent boy in our school. He went on to say that if there was only one place available at Normanton Grammar School, Steven would be given it. They must have been filled with pride for what their son had achieved in a short amount of time in education.

However Steven wasn't happy about leaving the rest of his friends to go to the local secondary modern school. While we shared those special years together at Slack Lane Primary School we achieved something that the school has never again been able to replicate: we won the Yorkshire Cup for football. We played our hearts out and gave everything to bring that cup back to our little school. The photo below shows one of my greatest moments in life. Steve Tottey can be seen holding the cup below. Steve was our captain, and we all followed his advice. That's probably why we returned back with the pride of Yorkshire.

The Yorkshire cup. Fantastic feeling. The greatest memory I have of that final match was Steve Tottey's goal from the halfway line. I was standing next to him when he looked up and observed that the opposition goalkeeper was too far off his line. Steve didn't hesitate – he lobbed the ball straight over the keeper. I will always admire his strength and foresight, and his ability to command his team. Steve will always remain a close friend.

After that moment, trophies and days to remember were very few, but I do have fond memories of inter-village football tournaments taking place. They would normally be played on Saturday or Sunday. A player from Shay Lane or Down Crofton would see one of us from New Crofton/Lump and ask if we fancied a match. The answer was always yes. We would meet on the junior school pitch or the secondary modern pitch at the arranged time. None of us had the same strip, so on one team you would have Leeds, Arsenal, Sheffield Wednesday, and Manchester United shirts. However we had all grown up together, so every member of every team knew who was playing on their team. But looking back, I bet it was bloody confusing for anyone watching.

The matches sometimes went on for three hours, and we never ran out of energy. On one occasion our team had just won a corner, and Alan Thomas and I were running from the halfway line to get into the area for the cross. As we got to the edge of the area, Alan fell down, so I went over to him and started pulling his Leeds United shirt, saying 'come on Alan, we're going to miss this corner'.

At that point I noticed Alan was chewing the grass. I knew there was a problem, but I didn't know what, so, caring soul that I am, I left him there eating grass while I tried to help out with the more important job of seeing to the corner.

We wasted the corner and I decided to go back to look at Alan. He was coming around at this point. It appears he had just suffered his first and last epileptic fit. I felt really bad having left him, but you have to remember that I could have clinched the match for our team with that corner.

Then Alan said, 'Thanks for staying with me, Kev'. I thought, Alan doesn't remember me going for the corner. So I didn't make him any wiser. I just said 'I'm here for you mate, not a bloody corner' (good answer, I thought).

With that incident we all said it was time to call the match off and for me to take Alan home. As it happens we did beat Down Crofton 2-1. Whether we would have beaten them if it had gone the distance is another matter.

When I got home with Alan, I told his mother, Mabel, that he'd had a funny do on the pitch. She was about as sympathetic as a king cobra with a rat. She was the local gossip and on many occasions she would be sitting in our kitchen talking to my mother and I would grab a slice of bread and dripping and a drink of pop, then about turn and leave before Mabel started involving me in the conversation, because that woman could make your ears bleed with the constant chat.

Once I escaped through the back door I would heave a big sigh of relief. While walking up the path all I could hear was Mabel waffling on and laughing. I knew she would be tying my mother up for around two hours, so most times I would go over to my mates Tink (John) Taylor or we would head off bird-nesting – we usually went to Nostell Dam. Tink and I would lose all track of time. We'd climb trees, barns, rock faces – you name it, we would climb it. We'd risk life and limb for a bloody bird's egg.

Once we had taken the egg from the nest we then had to blow the yolk out of it to stop it going off. Now to do this task you had to select a lovely sharp hawthorn, then pierce both ends of the egg, put the fat end of the egg to your mouth and blow the yolk out, then pop the egg in a safe pocket in your coat. These eggs were treasured. Over the years me and Tink collected 106 different birds' eggs and kept them in a big box with flour in the bottom to keep them safe and sound. In the 70s it was still legal to collect birds' eggs, but it's totally illegal today and I agree with that. When I look back I think with great sadness how badly me and Tink treated those poor little birds. In our defence, we never removed any eggs unless there were more than four in a nest, because we believed a bird counts its eggs with its claws. They would be quite happy to sit back on the eggs and many times Tink and I would revisit the nest to make sure the eggs were hatched off successfully and the chicks were growing in the nest. So we did show compassion, without really knowing we were.

Many times we would be so engrossed in searching for more nests that the darkness would creep up on us. Before we knew what time it was we'd be lucky see our watches, it was that bloody dark. Tink, being the oldest, would make the decision to head back home, and I would be relieved because I would be starving by now, with a pocket full of eggs that I needed to get back safely.

Walking home, we would chat and laugh about friends and family. Tink came from a family of nine, and believe me they were all characters. He had three sets of twins in the family – he wasn't one himself, but he had enough knowledge for two. Tink knew more jokes than any comedian I've ever met – he was so funny and entertaining it was a pleasure to be mates and spend time with him, a friend you could never replace.

His dad, Fred Taylor, was such a character – he used to wear wellies and a brown beret, even if it was summer. He would come out to us young lads who were playing football in the street and say 'come on, pass that ball'. We would kick the ball to Fred and he would dribble around the lads and do a running commentary, saying 'Geoff

Hurst going for goal passes to Martin Peters, who is looking for his first goal today', then when he was in position he would shoot in his wellies and invariably score. Then he would celebrate like a young professional footballer. He was great, such a laugh.

During the day Fred worked on the local farms, which he did until was 65 years old, when sadly he was told he had to retire. However he didn't want to. He kept going down to the farm and asking for work, but the farmer wouldn't let him because he was too old. Then one day Fred couldn't take anymore of not working. He went down to the train tracks and stood in the middle of the track with his head bowed to meet the next train head on. The train came, and that was the last we all saw of Fred. He was a great husband and father, a great person.

Things were never the same again in the street after Fred died. Tink and his family moved to Ryhill, leaving a massive hole in my childhood. However I can't start to think how big the hole was that Fred left behind in the Taylor household. When Fred took his own lovely life I was 12 or 13 years old. At that point I couldn't get my head around why someone would do that, but now I've experienced working life for the last 43 years and hit my own depression and mood swings head on. I now feel confident about the reasons Fred took his life in that way. On occasion, suicide has not been far from my own mind. It's a very dark place to visit. However I've resisted the urges and the callings of my mind to carry out the final act.

You would think after someone as special as Fred had taken his own life, the community would grind to a halt. But as we did in those days, we just moved on with our lives. Times were hard, but there was always something around the corner for kids.

The next big challenge came when it was time to move from our lovely little junior school to a huge secondary school. Kids came from three surrounding villages, Streethouse, Walton and Sharlston. This was a very eventful time, as you were all thrown together in a massive playground, and that spelt trouble from the off. Fights broke out all over the playground, to be stopped and broken up by the teachers. Then you would be sent straight to the headmaster, who didn't suffer fools. You would be dealt with by way of the stick. I received one crack with the stick on each hand on my first day. I thought, is this for real? And it bloody hurt.

As time went on we all settled down and found our own pecking order. The bullying in the seventies was unbelievable, and it was never addressed by the teachers, so there was only one way forward. You didn't back down; you stood your ground. Even if it was the top boy in the school, you had to try not to look a little weed, even though you got a good hiding in the end. But hey ho, you didn't back down.

Me and a band of roughnecks bonded together and watched each other's backs for the next five years. Steven Totty would sneak into our school with us from the grammar school and sit in classes. Teachers would ask on occasion, 'who are you?' Steven would reply 'I've just started here, miss,' and we would back up his story. It got to a point where he was spending more time at the secondary modern than most of the rest of us. He even played football with our team, and again no questions were asked. This situation was so funny. But Steven still passed all his exams with flying colours, and yes, at the grammar school, not the local secondary modern.

In those days there was so many characters. The teachers in the secondary modern were like the ones in the 1970s TV series 'Please Sir'. The RE teacher was just like Mr Hedgers and the Humanities teacher was just like Taffy. All we did all day long was enjoy the entertainment they supplied. The Humanities teacher was Mr Roberts, and that guy was one on his own. He would walk in class with a cigarette in his hand and say, 'Come on chaps, it's time to feed the hens'. He only said things like that because he didn't want to do any paperwork – crafty old bugger.

He had bred a cockerel that stood three foot high, or to you modern guys, one metre. That bird was so angry that no one dared to step into the compound. Then one day Mr Roberts asked me to collect the eggs from the nest boxes. I said 'yes, no problem sir'. All my mates started to say 'Oh my god, what you going to do with Hercules?' (That was the cockerel's name.) I replied, 'Come and watch me, I'll get them bloody eggs if it kills me'.

Off we went, and I picked up a metal bar outside the metalwork shop. All the guys said, 'you're never going to use that, are you?' I said, 'if that bloody thing attacks me, it's getting some'.

With that I entered the hen run, and there he stood. His chest was massive. I tried to shoo him off, but to no avail. He stood proud and tall, and I entered like a matador, except I had an iron bar, not a cape and a sword. He looked at me and flapped his wings, then he ran at me and jumped on my head, pecking my face and head, and it bloody hurt. So I grabbed him and threw him to the floor. He came straight back at me, so I hit him with the iron bar straight round the head. He immediately fell to the floor, and I thought I had killed him. All my mates were cheering.

With him out of it, I proceeded to the egg boxes to retrieve the eggs, but all of a sudden he was on my neck again from the back. He had his claws in my neck and he was pecking my head. So this time he was going to get what he deserved – that bloody cockerel was a real villain. I grabbed him by the neck and threw him over the fence, gathered the eggs real quick, then ran out of the compound. I had just shut the gate when Hercules flew back into the compound. I never faced that bloody thing again.

However, walking the streets was very similar to entering that cockerel's domain. In mining communities the priority was to learn how to look after yourself and defend yourself. These communities could be dangerous places. Large families would very often control villages with fear and violence. As a young male you had to make your mark on the village. I learnt this at a young age. I attributed the hatred I had been shown by my siblings to my disregard for the ruling rough families within the village.

I soon began fighting, and gained respect from the older and harder members of the village. I was no longer the younger brother of my three siblings. I was someone who you didn't cross.

As time moved on and I grew bigger and stronger, my brothers started to back off. They knew that if pushed it would take away any respect they had within the community. I would have fought with them if that was the case.

CHAPTER 2

Earning a crust

—◦∞◦—

Both my brothers joined the Merchant Navy and saw the world. I was pleased when they left home, for lots of reasons. One was that Trevor used to come to bed and scare me to death. He would walk in the bedroom pretending to be Frankenstein. Once I nearly started crying. He was afraid Dad would come and see what was going on, so he would get in bed and be nice to me. Eventually we would drift off to sleep. Then in came Melvin, who would throw the window open because he had bad asthma. Then during the night I would wake up with no covers on me because the two of them had pinched them. I would grapple with the covers trying to get covered up and warm again. Finally I would fall to sleep. Then nine times out of ten Trevor and I would wake up wet through, due to Melvin peeing in the bed. Mother would come flying into the bedroom. Shouting, 'What the bloody hell's going on here?' Melvin would be all apologetic, but mother still gave him a hard time. It wasn't nice to be in a wet bed, but I still think mam was wrong to tell him off. They were long nights.

It was lovely to sleep alone for the first time in my short life and it was also lovely to see the backs of those two hotheads. However, my sister Christine was still at home. She behaved like my second mother when it suited her. She was seeing a local lad called Brian Woodcock. Brian was Mr Grumpy – he never had a good word for anyone, especially me. We were to clash big time further down the line.

When Brian called round to our house my dad would be working and my mother would be out seeing her fancy man, Eric, so the first thing these two young people head over heels in love had to do was... yes, you guessed it, get rid of me. It might be only be six o'clock but I had to get up that wooden hill or feel the wrath of my sister. I preferred the first option.

These nights with Brian became a regular thing. Then one night I noticed my sister's belly was getting rather big, and let me tell you, it wasn't with too many Yorkshire puddings. So the next job was arranging their wedding day. What a bloody carry on that was. The day of the wedding I was there as page boy, and my two brothers were guests. My mother and dad looked like two corned beef inspectors. I've never seen them so smart.

After the ceremony, Christine and Brian moved in to their pit house at no. 8 Fifth Street, next door to Rose Fenn and Dave, her husband – they were a lovely family. Rose always had a big smile on her face. She went on to have five baby boys (not all at one go).

The first boy was called Graham and had been born in April '59, just before me, so we went through infant school and junior school together. It was only when we were going into the secondary school that Rose asked to speak to me, so I went to her house to ask what the problem was. There was a long pause, and then she went on to say, 'When you go to the secondary modern, please look out for our Graham'.

I was confused and said, 'Why, Mrs Fenn?'

She smiled at me and said, 'Graham is different to you Kevin, so please look after him, won't you?' So I said 'Yes, of course I will'.

She thanked me and I left. I must say I had no idea what she was referring to. However from day one I watched out for him. By the time we got into the third year at the secondary modem all the kids got the message: mess with Graham and you mess with me. And by this time all the lads were very weary of me. I think by the time I reached sixteen I realised why I was protecting Graham. He was gay. He always remembered me for those five years of unpaid protection. He became a highly successful hairdresser, but he never forgot me or his roots.

He met his long-time lover in his youth, a man called Lesley. He was a very successful businessman who went on to build a hairdressing empire for Graham. They were a very loving and emotional couple, but one day they would be on cloud nine and the next they would be fighting like cat and dog. They built various businesses up, but sadly lost them, although they were in a comfortable position. Then, one morning, Graham got up and as usual jumped in the shower. Lesley heard a loud crash, so he shouted, 'Graham, you ok?' No reply, so Lesley investigated. To his shock, he found Graham collapsed in the shower. He had suffered a massive heart attack. Lesley tried relentlessly to resuscitate Graham, but sadly there was no response. Graham was a large part of my childhood and hopefully I was a big part of his. I will always remember him for his humour, his direct way of speaking and the love he gave endlessly to his mother. God bless him.

But to return to the story that brought us together as friends. It started when my sister spent time next door to this wonderful family. Time moves on and people don't stay in one house, and they had moved by the time my nephew was born.

They named him Bryan Harvey Woodcock. He was a lovely little lad, and bonny. I always remember how Christine once bought Bryan some little red wellies. He loved them so much he refused to take them off for bed, so to stop him getting upset before he went to bed, Christine would put him in bed with the wellies over his pyjamas. Then when he was fast asleep she would sneak into his bedroom and remove the wellies. It was so funny to see and to witness my sister on edge so much. That little lad ruled her life from the day he was born, and she ran round after him like a trained nanny. Maybe she did her training with me. She put the time in, with me and her husband Brian. She turned into a wonderful mother and gave little Bryan all her time and love over the years.

As time rolled on and the years flew past, by the time I was eleven years old I was commanding respect within the community. This may appear strange, but let me assure you I never wanted to appear some kind of bully. It wasn't a label that was given to me. I just stood my ground and defied those who wanted to cross the line of tolerance.

Many things happened in the 70s, but one of the worst and most stressful times was in 1972, when there was a miners' strike. At this time I was twelve years old. We had to dig coal out of railway bankings, using old picks and shovels. When we bagged the coal, we thought, How do we get this bloody coal home now? Think on – I'm only twelve and the site we're digging on is a mile away from home. The only way to get the coal home was to ask one of the men who had a car to take it.

Now this was 1972, in the middle of a very nasty strike, and not many people owned cars or vans; Push bikes were the usual form of transport. So anyone lucky enough to own a vehicle could demand sacks of coal for transporting it home.

One such guy was my next door neighbour, Scotch Jim. He would take a bag of coal as payment for taking my coal home. At the time I thought this was a great deal, but as I have grown up I realise Scotch Jim was lifting my leg. He had to go home himself at some point, so really he was getting a free bag of coal for driving home. But he was a hard-working man who was just trying to keep is family warm, same as the rest of us.

So we children were digging into railway bankings for fuel to keep warm. It was so dangerous that looking back, I'm surprised none of us were killed.

That winter of 1972 went on forever. We burned anything we could get our hands on, including farm fences, old shoes, sheds, even tyres. There were power cuts every night – at 6 pm the electricity went off, and the street lights. If you were unlucky enough to be out at a friend's house after 6 pm, then you were in trouble. You now had to walk home in total darkness, feeling fences, hedges and even familiar cars to find your bearings and get yourself home. And once home, you could guarantee a good hiding for being late, and causing your mother distress.

Finally that bloody strike ended and my father returned to work. The lights went on and life returned to normal. Everyone tried so hard to put this time behind themselves, but one year on strike without money coming into the household made life so hard. By that time everyone was in debt and having problems with their family life. However, these people were known for their resilience and their strength as a community. Every one of them worked extra shifts at the pits and paid off their debts until once again they could look after their families. These guys were special, and as kids we all looked up to them.

Life started to creep back to the family life we had known before. While my mam and dad had gone through this bloody nightmare, my brothers were sailing around the world and getting paid for their comfortable jobs. I bet they were living like movie stars, while we were shivering like turkeys at Christmas.

Below is a picture of my dad and his mates at Walton Colliery. They look like a great team of pit lads. Dad is standing back left as you look at the picture.

My brothers would on occasion return home on leave from the Merchant Navy, though Mother would hope they didn't get leave together, as this spelt trouble.

I remember one such occasion when they both came home after a long time at sea. It was like throwing a match into a box of fireworks.

My father was always working or at the betting office, so my mother was the person who had to deal with everything, from cooking, cleaning, washing and ironing to being a professional referee. Once these two idiots called brothers had grown tired of knocking lumps out of one another, they would turn their attentions to me, sending me on errands to the shop to ask friends if they were going for drinks in the local pubs. Remember there were no mobile phones then and very few people had telephones in their homes.

To young people today, that would be like cutting their right hand off. The way we communicated in those days was the way the cavemen did. We walked to the people we needed to speak to, and then talked to them.

Today we see more and more youngsters walking around like drones, one hand held out with mobile phone placed firmly in it, head down, looking at the rubbish constantly coming through on social media.

So thank God I was brought up in a generation that never had fun with mobile phones. However, we had people who were economical with the truth and their intentions. The next recollection proves that last statement.

One day, old Tommy Davis walked to our house to ask me if I fancied owning a piglet. Straight away I said yes, obviously I would love to own a piglet.

He said 'well, I would like you to chop sticks every night after school with my grandson, Who I believe you go to school with'. I replied, 'do you mean Tony Davis?' He said 'yes, he chops sticks every night after school. Then on a Saturday I'll need you to help our Tony sell the sticks around the Lump.'

The Lump was an area of around 300 pit houses. This was a dream of a place to sell sticks because every house had a coal fire, so everyone needed sticks to light the fire. Old Tommy was the first entrepreneur I ever met. If the Dragons' Den had been around then, Tommy would have probably sold Peter Jones a piglet.

Anyway, back to Tommy and his slave trade. Every night I went chopping sticks – and chopping fingers. I think I hit my bloody fingers more than I ever hit the wood I was making sticks out of. Tony and I would parcel the sticks up every night and put them on the handcart. By Saturday the cart would be full and me and Tony would set off pulling the cart between us both. We would walk up and down every street on the Lump knocking on all the doors and asking if the householder if they would like to buy sticks. Some people would be pleasant and cheerful, and then you would get the other end of the spectrum. These people would argue about the price, the wrapping and the origin of the wood. A bag of these sticks was sixpence, or 2.5 new pence. Both of us had got a handful of plasters and legs that felt like jelly after pulling this big heavy cart full of sticks around 300 houses, yet this caveman still wanted the bloody sticks cheaper. There was more chance of the Pope turning Jewish than us letting these hard-won sticks go cheap. Besides, we had Old Tommy to answer to when we returned to the allotment with the empty cart and a bag of money. So we would say to the caveman, 'sorry, Tommy says you pay or we walk away, so it's up to you'.

At this point there would be a Mexican stand-off. We would all stare at one another, then Tony and I would say 'come on let's move on', and at that point the caveman would say 'okay, sell me two bags but make them the biggest ones'. He was still trying to get value for money. So I would say 'well you pick them', and straight away he would rifle through the whole cart full of sticks. In all honesty he probably got six sticks more than if I had passed him two at random. Some people you just can't please.

Once we returned Tommy would say, 'well done lads, where's the money?' but I think he got his greetings the wrong way round. He meant to say 'where's the money?' first and then 'well done lads'. That was Tommy. He could split a pea in two or peel a orange in his pocket with a boxing glove on. God he was tight with money. He never gave me or Tony any money; we had to wait for the piglets to be born. When the sow had the piglets she had 12, so that night after school Tommy asked me and Tony to pick one. We were so excited. Tony picked his and I went next and picked mine.

Every night we would chop the sticks and then play with the piglets, until the sow got fed up with our presence. At that point you knew it was time to leave before she took her frustrations out on you. Anyway we would arrive at the allotment around the same time every night and chop sticks and hands for about two hours, then play with the pigs. Notice I've started saying 'pigs', because the little piglets were now pigs. So me and Tony talked about asking his Grandad Tommy to take the pigs to market and at that point we would receive the money for chopping around six million sticks and dragging that bloody heavy cart around all the houses.

So we agreed that the very next night when we met at the allotment, we would ask Tommy to arrange for the pigs to go to market. When we met at the allotment, Tommy was standing at the gate and he appeared to be upset. So I said, 'are you okay Tommy?'

He looked at me and shook his head. Then he said, 'it's the pigs, lads'.

So me and Tony looked at each other and said to Tommy, 'what's wrong Tommy? He replied, 'they're all dead'.

I said, 'what, all of them?'

He replied, 'yes, even the mother'.

We were devastated. After the initial shock, I said, 'where are the bodies?'

Tommy started to get a little flustered. 'Er er er... I had to burn them and then I buried them in case of any infection for the other livestock'. At the time Tommy was very convincing but I'm sure you have worked out already that Tommy, the bloody old tightarse, had taken the sow and her piglets to market for a nice little pay day for him and his wife. So me and Tony got absolutely nothing for all that hard work over a period of approximately six months.

Needless to say, both of us stopped the sticking job, and Tommy moved on to the next two mugs.

The moral of this story is clear. Working for nothing will put nothing on the table. Tommy, God rest your soul. But when it's time for me to join you behind the pearly gates, remember there's an outstanding debt – one piglet.

The experience with Old Tommy didn't put a stop to my young ambition to earn money.

During these days as an eleven or twelve-year-old lad you only had money in your pocket if you worked. So I went back to the drawing board and gave consideration to a number of ideas.

Then all of a sudden, while I was sitting at the entrance to the Lump with bugger all in my pocket, a coal wagon came past me with three sections on the back of the van, each with a ton of coal in it. The driver would deliver a ton to each and every house on the Lump, because all the men who lived in the houses worked at the surrounding pits, so every day these three wagons would drive to three houses and drop the coal outside their coal houses at the back.

I thought to myself, I need a bloody coal shovel. This is where I will turn a coin. So I went looking around for a shovel.

As I was passing Tart Turner's allotment, I spotted a coal shovel. Now I knew Tart had a few of these shovels, because he bagged and sold coal all over Yorkshire. So I thought, this can be Tart's contribution to my coal-shovelling career. In other words, I nicked it.

I dashed into his allotment, grabbed the shovel and made my escape through the corn field. Luckily, no one spotted me. As I exited the field I brushed myself down, put the shovel over my shoulder and walked back down to the Lump.

I knocked on the first door where the coal had been delivered. Mrs Garforth opened the door immediately and I said, 'Could I get your coal in Mrs Garforth?' She replied, how much love? I hadn't thought of a price.' so I quickly said 'Twenty-five shillings please'.

She raised an eyebrow and said, 'ok love, get on with it'.

I was so excited I threw the square coal house door open and started throwing the coal through the small door, which was about four feet off the floor. Now at this point I'm about five foot five inches high and weighing around ten stone, so as you can imagine, after throwing about 3/4 of a ton of coal four feet through a little hole in a wall, I was knackered. But I stopped wiping my head, which was dripping with sweat. The last six shovelfuls felt like they weighed a ton each.

Once the coal had been thrown into the coal house, you had to sweep the dust up and throw that in. Then the moment I had waited for. Knock knock...

Mrs Garforth answered the door. She said 'thank you' love' and passed me 25 shillings.

I went straight to the top shop, better known as Alf Hill's. I bought a bottle of pop and a Mars bar. At this point my hands, arms, and back were killing me, but life was looking up.

As I was sitting on the wall relaxing, my Uncle Bill was on his way to Alf Hill's. He spotted me with the shovel and asked what was I doing with it.

I replied, 'I'm getting coal in for people on the Lump'.

He said, 'How much are you charging?'

I said 'Twenty-five shillings'.

He said 'Get yourself down to our house, there's a ton of coal just been delivered'. He dug in his pocket and pulled out 25 shillings. 'Go on. Get yourself off.'

At that, I picked up my shovel and off I went to Uncle Bill's house. I was bloody dreading it. Every bloody bone in my body was hurting. But you can't make a omelette without breaking eggs.

When I arrived at the house I put my big bottle of pop in the corner so it didn't get broken by flying pieces of coal. I looked at the mound of coal and thought, 'is this a good idea?'

With that thought I threw the little coalhouse door open and started shovelling. By the time I got to the end of the Black Death experience known as coal, I was sweating like a turkey at Christmas.

I swept up and locked up. Then I knocked on the door and my Auntie Gladys answered it and said, 'Hello love, what have you been doing?'

I explained about my new venture. She said 'Oooh love, are you sure about this kind of work? It's heavy work for a little lad like you.'

'I know Aunt Glad, but I need to earn money, and what else can I do?'

She said, 'Has Uncle Bill paid you?' I said 'Yes, he was going in Alf Hill's when he spoke to me.'

She said, 'Did he have his slippers on?' I said yes.

'He's gone bloody drinking in that back room at Alf's,' she said. 'Wait till I see him! Anyway, thank you Kevin, say hello to your mam from me.'

'Okay Aunt Glad.'

I walked off thinking I should have said he had his shoes on, not his slippers. I bet he got a right ear bashing when he returned from Alf Hill's slipper club.

When I got home my mother said. 'How come you're so bloody black, and where did you get got that shovel from?'

I told her what I'd been doing and how much I had earned. She said again, 'So where has that shovel come from?'

I didn't want to answer, but she kept asking. So I said it was stood doing nothing at Tart Turner's allotment so I picked it up.

'You are bloody joking, Kevin?'

'No, that's were I got it from.'

'Tart'll go chuffing mad when he finds out who's got it. Go to his house and apologise and ask if you can buy it off him.'

As I turned around to leave, I felt a smack around the back of my head. 'Get down there now!' she shouted.

I rubbed my head and set off. When I arrived at Tart's house I was shaking in my boots because at this point I realised I had really stolen the shovel, and that had consequences.

I knocked on the door and Tart answered. 'Hey up young 'un, what can I do for you?'

I swallowed what felt like a Jaffa and said, 'I picked up this shovel from your allotment Mr Turner and went throwing coal in for people on the Lump'.

He said, 'Did you get some work lad?'

I said 'Yes, at Mrs Garforth's and my Aunt Glad's'.

He smiled and said. 'You keep that shovel lad, it sounds like you need it, and I don't.'

I thanked him and told him my mam had made me come down to apologise. He said 'She was right to tell you to come down. And now because of your honesty, you've got yourself a fine coal shovel. But don't ever go in my allotment again or I'll be upset, and you don't want that do you?'

I stood in front of him shaking and said, 'I will never go in the allotment ever again'.

He rubbed my head, said 'good lad' and shut the door. I breathed a sigh of relief and walked back home with my shovel over my shoulder. I could now carry it with pride.

On my return my mother was waiting for me. As I walked in the back door she stood in front of me with her arms folded. She said, 'What happened? What did he say?'

I said 'Mr Turner was really nice. He told me to keep the shovel because he thought I needed it more than he did'.

'Did you go to the right house? Because I've never known Tart be that nice when someone pinches off him.'

I said obviously I had been to the right house. Mother said 'Well, I'll see him in the miners' welfare tonight, so you'd better be telling the truth.' She looked at the shovel and said, 'Put that bloody shovel in the coal house for God's sake'.

She met up with Tart later in the welfare that night and he confirmed my story and said I was a lad trying to earn money in a environment that didn't give it away. When mother spoke to me the next day, she apologised and gave me a kiss. My chest was stuck out like a bantam cockerel.

I carried on with my coal shovelling job for about twelve months – and then disaster hit our happy home. My father found out that my mother was having an affair, with a local man. Their marriage had been violent to say the least, but now this new revelation had lifted its ugly head.

I was upset and crying in my bedroom. I knew it was only a matter of time before more violence would ensue. Sure enough it was Saturday night, and my mother had gone to the local miners' welfare. She was late home that night, but my father was sat up waiting for her.

As soon as she walked through the door he started shouting, calling her everything from a whore to a slag. I remember sitting shaking and sobbing in my bedroom. Then I heard them on the stairs arguing. In an attempt to stop them, I ran out of my bedroom, pleading for them to stop. My father told me to get back in my room, and just as he was talking to me my mother hit him over the head with the poker from the fireplace. He turned and punched mother in the face, and she fell down every step of the staircase. I heard her crying and shouting abuse at my dad.

That night seemed to last forever. It was the kind of night you have nightmares about – I still do.

The next day my mother was bruised and limping. Dad was quiet but still full of hell. He was a proud man and a good dad, but things had gone to crazy for this quiet man from North Yorkshire.

Soon after this incident, Dad was rushed into hospital with kidney stones. He stayed in hospital about three weeks. While he was in hospital, talk about while the cat's away...

My mother would leave me around 7. 30 pm to meet her fancy

man. She wouldn't return sometimes until 2 am. One night I was so scared that I sat with my pellet gun loaded and my pet dog on my knee. At around 1 am I thought I heard her walking down the path, so I decided to open the curtains. Big mistake, because there was a man stood staring in through the window. I was terrified. Even now, typing this, the hairs on the back of my neck have lifted.

I recognised the man – he was a strange man who lived alone in the pit houses. When my mother came home I told her about this incident.

She said, 'Don't be silly, Mr Darwell wouldn't come up here at this time of night.'

Looking back, he was probably planning to try his luck with my mother, but unluckily for him there was someone in the house, a very scared little boy.

My dad came home after about three weeks. I was so pleased to see him I gave him a hug, and in mining communities in the 70s boys didn't hug dads. Dad looked really shocked, as I had never done that before, but in a way I think he knew why I hugged him like that.

He was a man who didn't suffer fools, but he knew when someone was taking him for a ride, ie my mother. On many occasions after the operation he would ask me what had happened when he was in hospital. I always replied 'Nothing dad, mum didn't even go out'.

I knew this was lies, and it was wrong, but I loved my dad very much. To tell him what had really happened in those three weeks in 1972 would have ripped his heart out. I couldn't do that. Unlike my mother, I loved him too much.

Within weeks things got worse – more fights, more arguments, more sleepless nights for me. Then one day I came home from school and my dad was sitting in his chair. He looked at me with tears in his eyes and said, 'Tomorrow you and me are leaving this house and your mother'.

For once I was speechless. He said, 'Are you OK Kevin?'

I replied, 'Where are we going dad?'

He said, 'I've bought our Christine's house.'

I started to say, 'I don't really want to leave mum...' but Dad broke me off halfway through the sentence. 'There's no choice Kevin, you're coming with me.'

The next morning a van turned up to move us to our new home. The guy who moved us was a local jack the lad called Herbert Greatorex. Dad tried his best to soften the blow for me. He could see I was crying – he really was a great bloke. With everything now in the van, Dad said, 'Say goodbye to your mum'.

She kissed me and said, 'you will always be welcome here'. I kissed her, crying, distressed, and very worried for the future.

My dad was shouting 'Come on, we need to go'. I looked at mum with tears in my eyes and said, 'I don't want to live with dad'.

She said, 'Go on Kevin, your dad's waiting'.

At that point I realised I had been a mistake. I had become a nuisance, something the two of them were stuck with. I felt rejected by my mother.

I turned and walked down the path towards Dad and Herbert, with his van that moved everything and everybody within the Crofton boundaries. I looked back at our family home, where so many memories were. I remember thinking, how will I cope without my mother? Then I heard Dad's voice in the background: "Come on Kevin, Herbert's busy this morning."

I climbed into the van, with Herbert driving. Ten minutes later we were pulling up outside my new home.

The next four years would be the strangest of wake-up calls. I would never be the same innocent young lad again.

CHAPTER 3

Living with Dad

—⧓—

The day I had to leave my mother and our home changed my life forever. I went from a young boy playing football and laughing with friends, a kid, to the person who was responsible for cooking, washing, ironing, dusting, and making sure the house ran like clockwork. All this for £1 a week pocket money. So in between I had to get a paper round to earn £1.50 a week. Then a milk round cropped up at £2.50 a week. Needless to say, to the paper round had to go.

Dad, on the other hand, didn't change his role at all. He went to work, came home, ate his dinner, then straight to the bookie's. There he would lose all his money, as he had done when living with my mother. When he returned, penniless, he would always blame anyone and everyone else for his stupidity.

He was a strict man and commanded respect from his family. Heaven knows how he did that, with the way he had treated our mother. Irrespective of her affair, she was still the woman who had borne his four children. However, Dad still commanded respect.

I would return home at the designated time of 9 pm. That time was not negotiable by even one minute. After burning just about everything, I managed to serve up some sort of meal for us.

Dad pulled me to one side and said, and I quote: 'Tomorrow, go and see the headmaster and tell him you want to drop woodwork and take up cookery'.

You can imagine my face. At this point in my school life I was one of the hardest boys in the school, and my dad was telling me to ask the headmaster to let me do cookery.

After the initial shock I replied: 'So why do I have to drop woodwork for cookery?'

Dad answered in a crack. He said, 'because we can't eat blocks of wood, lad'.

That's when I knew that life would never return to the way it was when Mum was with us.

The next day I approached the headmaster and told him of my situation. He agreed it was best all round. So that week I went into cookery. I felt so embarrassed, and my friends were ripping the life out of me. They would shout, 'what does Fanny Cradock think about it?' For those who where not born back then, Fanny Cradock was the modern-day equivalent of Gordon Ramsay.

After two or three weeks, things settled down. I began to enjoy it. One, I got to be among the girls, and obviously I was always interested in the female half of the population Two, I got to eat everything I made and eat others' cooking, if I didn't get caught. Dad started to enjoy my cooking a bit too much. He started to get fat.

There's a picture in the centre pages which shows me eyeing the veggie at the local show in 1973. There I stand with three good mates, Kevin McInerney, Tony Crossland and Stuart Pitchfork. Sadly, a few years later we lost Stuart. He had found love with a girl, but unfortunately she hadn't, and she broke it off. He couldn't take the split, so he decided to take his own life. Stuart (Matey) Pitchfork,

I loved you in life and believe me I will love you on the other side. God bless.

During my time at this school I had so many great times and laughed so much my ribs would be hurting. One incident that sticks in my mind was when me and my mate Johnny Scuffam decided to bunk off school and sit in my bedroom smoking and shooting my air rifle. Suddenly we heard a loud knock on our front door, so we sneaked into my dad's bedroom and looked down from his bedroom window. It was the bloody kiddie catcher. With that we dived to the floor and waited for him to leave. Then we laughed and resumed our naughty activities.

Later that day Johnny went home as though he had attended school. Then my father returned from work. He said 'Have you had a good day at school?' I replied 'Yes, been great Dad'. He then asked what lessons I had had. With that I started to rattle off the usual, Maths, English... My dad stopped me there and said. 'You bloody little liar. The school kiddie catcher came to my work because he said you and Scuffam were off school. He says you're off more than anyone else. So what are you playing at?'

I had to think on my feet. My reply was, 'We're not just bunking off school Dad, we're trying to find jobs for when we leave'. With that answer he calmed down and I was pleased he didn't give me a good hiding. He said, 'Start going to school, now'.

'Yes Dad.'

Then he just popped the kettle on.

Dad was a creature of habit. He worked whether he was poorly or not; sick leave wasn't for Dad. No, John Willie would walk to work if there were no buses. But his downfall in life was his gambling. As soon as Saturday came around he would have his reading glasses on and the paper open on the racing page. At this point you could not speak to Dad, he was so engrossed in the racing page. I would leave the house quietly and return when the racing day was done. Before I got home I would know what Dad's mood would be like. He would have lost all our money, and this left him seriously angry and upset. He knew this gambling was a big problem, but he had no idea how to control it. Gambling was to be the downfall of our life together.

Then out of the blue, a good mate of mine asked me if I would like a job at Mr Elsley's butcher's shop. I said 'What, do you want me to cut up cows?' He said 'Don't be daft, I'm talking about delivering meat and bread plus eggs. You get to ride the butcher's bike, and best of all you get paid.'

'How much?'

'Five pounds a week, but you only deliver on a Saturday. Friday nights you make sausage and pork pie fillings with me.'

I thought this sounded a good little number, so I said, 'OK mate, when do I start?'

Steve said, 'This Friday and Saturday.'

'Ok mate, no problem, I'll meet you at the butcher's on Friday.'

'Six o'clock.'

'No problem.'

I was really excited. When I told Dad, he looked astonished that I'd landed such a nice little job.

My first night was a complete laugh. We started making sausage meat, and once we had made the meat I was shown a bucket full of cold water and what looked like slime floating on the top. I asked Steve, 'What the bloody hell is that in the bucket?' He replied 'that's the sheep's intestines that make the skin for the sausage'.

He plunged his hand into the bucket, found the end of an intestine and placed it over the nozzle of the sausage maker. Then he set the sausage machine going and started to twist the intestine and make beautiful sausage. I asked him to give me a go. It was going great, until Steve turned up the flow. I couldn't twist the sausage quick enough, so I ended up with the biggest sausage you've ever seen. We laughed so hard both of us nearly wet ourselves.

Then the fun stopper came in (that's the butcher). 'What the bloody hell are you two playing at?' he said. We both said the sausage machine had gone into overdrive. He said 'Right, get that sausage meat sorted out, then make some pie mix.'

'Ok Mr Elsley.' We collected all the bits of meat that Mr Elsley had trimmed off in the shop that day. As we put them through the grinder we used a plastic plunger to push the meat through. All of a sudden a sparrow flew into the preparation area, and we tried to get it back out, but in the confusion the sparrow flew into the grinder and went straight through into the mix. Steve and I were frozen to the spot. We looked at one another and I said, 'Oh shit, what do we do now?'

Steve said, 'We'll have to throw the mix away.'

'Mr Elsley will go mad Steve, look how much mix there is. You can't even tell there's a sparrow in the mix, there's no sign of feathers because the grinder chewed everything so small.'

'OK, let's start filling the pies.'

We worked our fingers to the bone so all the pies would be filled and the lids placed on top before Mr Elsley came into the preparation area. Once we had got all the pies filled and lids on we placed them on the baking tray and asked Mr Elsley to bake them off. He came into the preparation area and said 'They look lovely pies lads', then he put them all into the oven and baked them off. When they came out, the first thing he did was eat one. He said 'You've done me proud lads, that pie's beautiful.' I thought, if you knew what was in it you wouldn't be saying that. Then Steve cracked a joke, just for me. He said, 'I bet them pies fly out this week, Mr Elsley'.

I was in stitches laughing. At this point Mr Elsley said, 'Don't you think they'll fly out, Kevin?'

I had to think on my feet quickly. So I said I thought Steve was referring to flying pigs, 'you know when someone is lying, sorry for laughing.'

He looked and said, 'Oh good, I thought there was a problem'.

We both piped up, 'no problem, Mr Elsley'.

With that he said 'OK Kevin, see you in the morning for the delivery round.'

'What time?'

'Nine o'clock lad.'

Off we went, laughing all the way home, saying we would never eat a pork pie from that shop again.

The next morning I reported for duty and Mr Elsley said, 'First of all I would like you to take these nineteen dozen eggs down Shay Lane. The addresses are in the basket with the eggs. Then come back to the shop for the meat deliveries.'

'No problem Mr Elsley.'

So off I went. Now to get to Shay Lane you have to go down the biggest hill in Yorkshire – it's called Church Hill. As I was navigating my way down the hill, dodging bricks and holes, I shouted 'hiya' to someone I knew. That was the biggest mistake I have ever made. The front wheel went into a pothole, and I shot over the handlebars and landed on my bottom. The bike and its contents were trashed. The bike was in a tangle and the eggs were the biggest omelette you've ever seen.

I picked up the bike and returned to the butcher's. Mr Elsley went mad. He gave me five pounds wages for the work I'd done over two days and said 'Don't both coming back Kevin. I don't think this job is for you.'

I was really fed up. Though I'd made a mess down Church Hill, it wasn't intentional. But that's life, and there were plenty more ups and downs to come in my life.

The prime example that springs to mind is the occasion when me and a friend called John Hawkhead from Foulby took on a little bit of land across from his house. We wanted hens so we could sell their eggs to make some pocket money. The only problem was that neither of us had any money, so how were we supposed to buy hens to make our first million? And come to think of it, what about a shed to keep them in? So we sat thinking and planning. Then all of a sudden I thought, there's a builders yard up the road called Abbot's. We decided to steal the wood we needed from the yard. So for the next seven nights we climbed through the wire fence, where we had cut a hole, to take the timber.

We both knew we were breaking the law and looking at a crack around the earhole off our dads if we got caught, but that dream of grandeur drove us both on night after night. After seven scary nights, we had lifted enough timber, so it was time to get building. We scrounged nails and a hammer and got weaving with the grand design for a hen hut. After about four days, the hut was completed. We made a good job of it, if I say so myself.

The next dilemma was how to fill the shed with hens. We were rather good at sneaking about after dark, so we started to cast our eyes over the nearby community of the Lump, an area of around 300 pit houses. There were lots of hens kept in the allotments there, and we decided to pay a visit to Mr Darwell and his flock. We got into the allotment at around 11 o'clock at night, lifted six hens off their perches and placed them in a large cardboard box, then walked back over the fields with our big box full of hens. We laughed and joked all the way back.

Once we reached our allotment we placed the hens on their perches in their new home, then locked up and went to our homes. We arranged to meet the next day and survey our ill-gotten gains. We rolled up at eight o'clock the next morning and opened the sheds up, and every one of them flew straight out of the open door. I thought we'd pinched six seagulls, not hens.

We gingerly looked inside the hut to make sure they had all gone, and to our surprise there were three newly laid eggs in the box. 'This is the start of our business,' said John.

The hens came back and that week we collected around two and a half dozen eggs and sold them. At last we had money in our pockets. But it wasn't to last. That night I slept at John's house. Early the next morning his sister Alma woke us both up and said 'John, there's a lovely policeman downstairs asking for you'. We now knew there were going to be consequences.

We jumped out of bed and got dressed in double quick time. When we peeped around the stairs we could see the local bobby. His name was Bobby Wood, and he was a tyrant. He curled his index finger and said, 'Come here you two, I've got questions for you'.

Me and John walked towards him with our heads bowed.

He said, 'Right you two, you've been pinching wood from Mr Abbot's yard'.

I said, 'What makes you think it's us, Mr Wood?'

'Because John is the only kid in this village with ginger hair. And where did those hens come from?'

We were lost for words. I had to think on my feet. I piped up, 'It's funny you should ask that question, Mr Wood. The hens walked over the fields and settled in our shed. John and I opened the shed door and the hens were sat there, so we assumed they had walked over the fields.'

He looked at me and said, 'You will now put those hens in a box and take them back to the rightful owner, Mr Darwell.'

I went to answer back, but Bobby Wood looked at me as if to say, 'Don't you dare say you didn't pinch them hens.'

I thought, Kev, keep your mouth shut, you're in enough trouble. So I said to John, 'I think it's time to put the hens in the box, John'.

'Good lad, Kevin,' said Bobby Wood.

So we reluctantly started to put the hens in the box. And the bloody hens were as reluctant as we were. Then we placed the box of hens in the police Ford Escort and me and John climbed in.

As we were travelling to the Lump to return the hens, I had a naughty thought. Why don't I open the box in the police car for the laugh? So I did. The hens flew all over the police car, shitting everywhere. Bobby Wood was shouting, 'Get them bloody birds back in the box!' I nearly weed myself. He was so mad.

When we got to Mr Darwell's, Bobby marched me and John to the house and introduced us as the hen rustlers.

Mr Darwell was not amused. He told us both, 'You're a pair of idiots, you should never take anything from people in the community.'

We both apologised and returned the hens to his allotment. He told Mr Wood, 'Bobby, don't prosecute these two, they're just lads'.

Bobby agreed and gave us both a bloody good telling off. And believe me, it worked.

Then he dropped a bomb on both of us. 'By the way, Mr Abbot would like to see you.'

So me and John got back in the police car and off we went to Mr Abbot's. On arrival he was standing in the driveway looking bloody upset. As we got out of the police car, Bobby Wood shouted, 'I'll leave these two in your care, Mr Abbot'. Mr Abbot looked at me and John and said 'Yes Mr Wood, I think that's the correct thing to do'.

With that Bobby Wood drove off.

By this time me and John were shitting ourselves. We had no idea how Mr Abbot was going to deal with us.

Then he said, 'Right, both of you in my office.' He pointed to the office door. We followed his instructions and walked in. He came in behind us and sat at his huge desk. 'Where is all my timber?' he barked.

I said, 'We built a shed with it, Mr Abbot, it's only just down the road from here.'

He smiled and said, 'Well that's good'.

John jumped in and said, 'Does that mean we can keep it, Mr Abbot?'

He looked at John and through gritted teeth he said, 'No lad, the reason I said it's good was you two idiots won't have far to bring it all back'.

I said 'We'll have to dismantle it, Mr Abbot'.

'Yes you will, and when you return it you will take every nail out first and place every piece on the same pile it came off.'

We looked at one another.

'If you don't complete this task by tomorrow I will inform Bobby Wood and he will have you both prosecuted. So it's your decision.'

I said, 'Is it ok if we leave now Mr Abbot and get started?'

He smiled and said, 'Now get out. Get my timber back here'.

We both apologised and walked out. We went straight to the allotment and started stripping the shed down. It took us all day and well into the night, but after hell of a lot of sweat and toil, we completed the job.

Mr Abbot said, 'If I ever see you two anywhere near my yard I will personally kick your arses. So get out of my sight NOW!'

We turned around and ran through the gates.

CHAPTER 4

Down the mine

———❧———

The next big dilemma was breaking free from state education. In 1975, when I turned sixteen, I left the local secondary modern school. All my friends were starting work on the Monday morning, and I think we officially left school on the Friday. So after twelve years of education we were expected to have just two days off, then start work. I thought no no, I'm having a little time off.

So when my dad said, 'when do you start work?' I replied, 'well, I thought I would have the six weeks of summer holiday off, then start'.

'I see, I thought you wouldn't want to work. You catch the bus to town and get a job now. If you don't get one, don't come home.'

So, very pissed off, I caught the bus to Wakefield. My first port of call was Citra, a soft drinks company, known for the Crystal Springs Soft Drinks Dispenser. Mr Woodhead, the manager, came and interviewed me. He said 'could you start Monday?' I panicked and said 'no, it would have to be Wednesday due to a bereavement'.

Mr Woodhead said 'That's ok, see you then Kevin.'

When I returned home, dad said 'Right, have you got a job?' I said yes. Dad looked astonished. He asked where, so I told him. Dad was really pleased. He even rubbed my head.

That five days soon passed, and I turned up on the Wednesday at 8 am and met the yard supervisor, Les Nixon. What a guy. He spoke to the workers like slaves and kept a sharp eye on all the young lads and drivers. I'm sure that man had been in the SS during WW2. He stalked around the factory and loading bays like a tiger, constantly watching what workers were up to. He never gave anyone a minute's peace. As soon as you stopped loading your lorry for the next day's deliveries, he would grab you by the collar of your jacket and place you on another lorry loading.

One day I'd just returned from a gruelling day on deliveries and I was knackered, so once I had loaded the lorry I sneaked off into the beer side, where lorries would be left parked up and sheeted ready for the next day. I opened the sheet on the back of the wagon and got underneath it. I managed to get comfortable in the middle of the next day's deliveries. However, the tiger was on the prowl. Mr Nixon had become suspicious about my whereabouts, so he started to look for me. I could hear him shouting 'Mr Graham, Mr Graham, where are you?'

I sat tight and hoped for the best, but he pulled the sheet back and saw me. He stood banging his board with his hand, shouting 'Come on Mr Graham, I've got more work for you than you could ever imagine'. He wasn't bloody wrong. He had me loading every available lorry in that yard. Come 5 pm I was out on my feet. Mr Nixon said to me as I was clocking off, 'You will be glad to get under your sheets tonight Mr Graham'. He was so right. I said 'I can't wait, Mr Nixon'. At that he rubbed my head and laughed. That was the first time he had shown any sense of humour.

The next day I was placed with a driver to do pop and beer deliveries. The guy was called Les Moore, and what a great guy. He made my work experience wonderful.

I stayed with these people and the company twelve months. Les and I delivered all over Leeds. It was hard work and poorly paid, but I loved it.

From Harehills to Seacroft, Les was a ladies' man. I remember a call we used to make in Harehills – Victoria Wines. The manager was a very attractive lady. Les would say to me after making the delivery, 'Kev, go get some fish and chips, I'm just going in for a chat'. I would reply, 'OK Les, whatever.' About 45 minutes later he would return to the van looking a little hot and bothered. He'd be smiling and looking at my face, then laugh and say 'what?'

The days of laughter and pleasure were endless.

The summer of 1976, that year I spent with Citra, was one of the hottest years in history, and the company couldn't make pop quick enough. I remember going into the factory to take hot quart bottles of orange pop off the production lines. While I was there, there were bottles exploding around me, due to the company trying to keep up with demand. However, the people who worked in the factory never bothered about bottles exploding. They just walked around like it was normal. On a couple of occasions I don't know whether I sat on a Mars bar or shat myself, but either way I had a little mess in my pants, thanks to the exploding bottles.

I never thought it was possible to deliver so much pop and beer in one day. I would return home after a shift in the cruel heat, and no sooner did I get through our front door than I'd drop in the chair and slam my feet up on the coffee table. Within seconds I would be fast asleep. Then, about an hour later, my legs would have gone numb. Trying to pull them off the table was like trying to remove two lumps of lead. When I tried to walk, I was like a toddler in a playpen. What an end to a day of laughter, graft and that bloody heat.

Once I got that summer of 1976 out of the way I started to think that although the job and the people I worked with were great, the wages didn't justify the amount of work that was expected from you as an individual. So it was time to cast the net a bit wider.

It wasn't long before something turned up. A friend of mine told me that Walton Colliery was taking on underground workers, so I called in at nine o'clock one Saturday morning. I spoke to the training officer, Joe Carroll. He asked me, 'Does yer dad work here?' I replied he did, and John Graham was his name. Joe said, 'He's a great guy and a good worker, so yes you've got a job. But first I need your NI number.'

I didn't know my NI number off the top of my head, so I replied 'sorry Mr Carroll, I can't remember it'. He looked up from the paperwork that he'd started and said, 'Right, it's now 9.30, and you've got until 12 noon to get back here with that NI number or you can kiss goodbye to your job.'

So now I had to run from Walton Colliery to my home on Slack Lane, Crofton. When I arrived home I was absolutely knackered. I searched around the house for my NI number and after about 15 minutes I found it. I looked at my watch. It was nearly 11.20. So I rushed out of the house. People were shouting 'What's the big rush, Kev?' I just waved and carried on running.

As I approached the shops I saw I a young kid getting on his shiny new pushbike, so I ran up to him and said 'I need your bike'. He looked shocked and said, 'It's new.' I said 'I'll return it back here for 2 pm'. He passed me the bike and I rode it like I was going for gold in an Olympic final.

I arrived at the training office at 11.50. Joe Carroll looked at his watch and said, 'You cut that a bit fine.' He took me into the office and signed me up.

And so I joined Walton Colliery in 1977, when I was eighteen years old.

On my first day down the pit I was walking down the working area when the man in front of me was hit on the top of the head with a lump of coal. I thought, 'Have I made the right move here?'

This job was to prove rewarding in the wages department, but it was about 100 times more dangerous than the exploding pop bottle factory. Accidents were commonplace. I witnessed a man losing his thumb – a big steel cable took it off like a hot knife through butter. He shouted, 'I knew I shouldn't have started early'. He grabbed his hand and shouted to me, 'Get the f***ing deputy to wrap this bastard hand up'. So I ran off and brought the deputy back with me (deputies were supervisors who carried first aid kits on their belts). The deputy who attended wrapped the guy's hand up like fish and chips and sent him out of the pit with a friend. That was a scary experience.

At the pit there were always accidents week on week, some minor and some major. Whenever I went down in the cage into the bowels of the earth, I feared being hurt, cut or killed. It was a very dangerous environment to work in. It was also a close-knit society, everyone watching everyone else's back. The older men would use their brains to get heavy jobs done without flexing their own muscles. They would see young fit lads walking into their gate underground, and you could see them thinking, today has just got better. They would shout 'lads, can you help me and my old guys out?' Knowing we dare not say no. So we'd say yes, how can we help? Then he would say, drag this cable into the gate.'

The cable and the brass pummel end weighed about a bloody ton. Me and the lads would tug and tow this monster of a cable about 100 metres. By the time we got it to where they wanted it, all of us would be knackered. The old guys would shake our hands and sit down, saying 'right fellers, after all that tugging and towing we've done it's time for our snap'. I used to think, you crafty buggers. Still, they were older guys who at some time were younger and they would have had the piss taken out of them then. That respect between us all was something to be proud of.

One day that sticks in my mind was a day I worked in the pit bottom. The deputy there was Harold Walker, a fiery little guy who took no shit from anyone. He lived three doors away from our family home and just by chance his daughter Elizabeth had been born the same day and year as me, so you can see we really did live in each other's pockets. Anyway, after we had got most of the mine cars full of coal out of the pit, Harold turned to me and said, 'Kevin, I'm going to send you up in the cage. Go to the canteen with this flask and ask them to fill it with soup'. I thought brilliant, I can have a fag, because smoking, for obvious reasons, was not allowed down the pits. The flask was huge, a good three feet tall.

I got on the cage with the flask and off I went. As soon as I hit the surface I borrowed a fag from the banksman, old Ken, then I ambled round to the canteen and asked Mrs Milligan to fill the flask with soup for the guys in the pit bottom. She replied in her Scottish accent, 'who the bloody hell told you to come and get this bloody thing filled?' So I replied that it was Harold Walker. She looked at the flask and said 'That little bleeder, this bloody flask is bigger than him'. She was a hard woman to please. Anyway, she filled the flask with tomato soup and off I went to the waiting cage. As I jumped on I saw old Ken the banksman laughing. The cage lifted up, Ken pulled the caller out from under it and then Geoff Thor (Thaw?), the winder, let the cage go at a speed he had never done before. The alarm went off on the cage, so it stopped in mid-shaft. The flask bust open and the soup went everywhere. I was covered in it. When Geoff got the cage moving again he took me down to the pit bottom and waited for me. All the lads plus Harold were creased up with laughter. I said 'you bastards set me up!' I had to work for five hours covered in tomato soup. What a day, and what a memory. Even when I came out of the pit after my shift, all them buggers on the pit top we're laughing. So cheers Geoff, Ken, Harold. And let's not forget the lads.

Every day someone had a prank played on them. As young lads we were still very boisterous, so even though we worked hard we still made time to do silly things that made us all roll about laughing. One day we decided to loosen the wheel nuts on a young lad's bike. A group of us young idiots watched and waited for this poor lad, John Conner, to set off home on his pushbike. He got his bike out of the bike shed and set off for home, only that wasn't going to happen. The wheels fell out of the frame and John was rolling around in pain.

Our laughter stopped when we saw that. We ran over to John and recovered him from the middle of the road. We all said sorry and helped him get his wheels back on. However this silly indiscretion had been observed by a pit official, who later reported it to the pit manager. This was not looking good for me and my Ryhill mates. We had to take the biggest roasting I think anybody ever received at Walton Colliery, but looking back, we did deserve it.

Pits were hard and dangerous places to work, but they were full of characters. The biggest character, and in my opinion one of the greatest union men I ever met, was Arthur Scargill. He took no shit from any member of management. He once came to Walton colliery and by accident I met up with him in the tailgate. He said to me, 'How are you, young man? You look a bloody fit lad', and smiled at me. I replied 'Cheers, Mr Scargill'. Straight away he said, it's not Mr Scargill, it's Arthur. I work for a living, not like the management'. He laughed.

As he joked with me the manager shouted 'Mr Scargill, could you hurry up please'. Arthur's face was a picture. He turned to the manager and said, 'I'm talking to a member of the NUM, so I will leave this young man when I'm ready'.

The manager just looked sheepishly at the floor. Then Arthur said, 'Right lad, I'm off before we end up with a strike on our hands'. He shook my hand and walk away with the down-trodden manager. To this day I admire that man. God bless Arthur Scargill.

My home life outside the pits was still up and down. My life with Dad wasn't looking good.

I kept house for Dad from the age of thirteen to eighteen, and our lives in those five turbulent and trying years brought us so close. However, my eighteenth birthday will always be remembered for the wrong reasons, because my friend Steve Totty's mother Bessie died two days before it. This was a massive blow for me as well as Steve, as Bessie had been like a mother to me over the past five years.

She and her husband Wally lived in a lovely bungalow on Hare Park Lane, Crofton. During the five years before her death, she would invite me round for tea and wouldn't spare any expense to feed me. At times I was so hungry I could have eaten two plates full of her lovely home-made steak pie and chips. But even then as a young lad I would show respect and courtesy.

Wally would cover the table with condiments, and Steve would comment regarding how many were on the table, and Wally would hit the celling shouting and bawling, 'if you don't bloody like it go eat somewhere else!' Steve would start laughing. Then Bessie would pop her head around the door and say 'Wally, shut the bloody hell up, our Steve is just getting you going, and he hasn't done a bad job, you silly old bugger'.

Then all through the meal Wally would be mumbling to himself, 'It's always me in the wrong, I'm bloody fed up with this family.'

When things like this happened, at first I would be embarrassed and feel as though I was intruding. But as those five years went on I just would laugh along with Steve and really enjoy the time I spent with this family that had taken to me like a second son. So as you can imagine, when Bessie died it was like losing a mother.

Bessie's body was brought back to the bungalow the night before she was buried in Crofton churchyard. Steve said, 'Will you come up to the bungalow Kev, to pay your last respects to my mam?'

I said 'Steve, I'm a little scared to say goodbye to your mam, I've never seen anyone dead'.

Steve said, 'My mam would be upset if you didn't pay your last respects'. Well, I would never ever upset Bessie, so I went with Steve up to the bungalow and he took me into his bedroom where Bessie was resting in her coffin. He removed the silk handkerchief covering her face.

It was so upsetting to see how that beautiful woman had gone from a laughing, chatting and loving person to a wizened old corpse. So, so sad. I cried and so did Steve, and I covered her once beautiful face up again with the silk handkerchief. Me and Steve hugged each other and shed a few tears.

The next day her burial took place at Crofton church. After the service and the interment we went to the wake in the working men's club at Crofton. This was a really sad occasion. Me, Steve and Johnny Scuffam used to stand in my dad's bedroom window and look into the club's tap room window. We could see members playing snooker on a table that was kept as well as any professional table. We would stand and dream about being eighteen and playing on that table. However, now that it was our time it was just too much like pleasure on the day Steve's mam died. We didn't go near that table. That day will stay in my heart forever.

Shortly after that earth-moving event my dad started to get involved with a woman in Wakefield called Mary Mercer. She was one woman I could not take a shine to. I found her rude and inconsiderate. It was my dad's decision if she was to be the woman he would stay with, but it would be a turning point in our lives. He announced to me that he was going to marry Mary, and said, 'You can come and live with us if you like'. I would rather have lived with Count Dracula. He wouldn't have taken so much blood. So I declined his offer. Then he said, 'Go and have a word with your mother and see if you can move back in with her.' He never explained that all this was because the house was being repossessed due to his gambling habit, and I was going to need a new home. At that time I was working down Walton pit, so I was earning enough money to get a mortgage on the house and save grace for me and Dad. But that never happened.

The day came when we said our goodbyes. The house was no longer ours. Dad shook hands with me and said, 'I hope everything works out back at your mum's'.

I told him not to worry, I would be fine, although I had no idea what was facing me.

Dad left, and me and my friends carried on our backs my bed, my belongings, and basically everything I had at that time to call mine. Imagine walking through the village you were born into and grown up in with all your worldly goods on show, your mattress on your head, your bedding and clothing in black bags.

Two mates from next door to my mother's house helped me return with all this baggage. A big thank you to Rob and Alan Jennings. But this was a very embarrassing time in my turbulent life.

Upon arrival at mother's I was welcomed with the words, 'You can stay if Eric says its ok'. Eric was her fancy man. At this point you can imagine how I'm feeling. Dad has moved on with his life, and mum has obviously moved on with hers. So that just leaves young Kev, who hasn't really moved on at all. In fact I have now returned to my childhood home, minus the man who for eighteen years I've looked up to, my dad.

It was time to meet the man who tore my life apart. What do we do in this instance? Should I be an ally to my father and make things difficult within the house, or do I behave and toe the line? I chose the latter. Just then, as a young man going into his eighteenth year, all I wanted was to move on, be happy, and forget this episode in my life.

I met Eric, and you know what? He was a nice bloke. We hit it off straight away. At times I remembered my childhood in the very same house I was now sharing with the man who had shafted that life. Even so, I couldn't bring myself to hate Eric.

I thought of all those nights my mum was unhappy and I looked at her now. My god, what a change. She beamed like the brightest light you have ever seen.

We all lived in harmony together for around twelve months, then one day our lives were once again turned upside down. Eric had been suffering from a sore throat for around two weeks. Finally mum told him to go to the doctor's, so he went on the Monday morning. Now usually you see the doctor, get a prescription and some medicine and return home. On this occasion, no such luck. The doctor told Eric to go home and get some pyjamas and go straight to Cookridge Hospital. That was the cancer hospital in west Yorkshire. It was a place to be revered.

Eric, mum and I all knew this was the beginning of the end. He spent about two weeks in Cookridge Hospital, and then they decided there was nothing more they could do for him, so home they sent him. He was never a big man, probably six foot tall and weighing about twelve stone, but when he returned home he had lost about three stone. He looked like a Japanese prisoner of war.

He slept in the front room and my mother slept on the settee. She was like an angel to Eric. She never left his side, and when he was in pain you could see she also was feeling that pain.

This situation went on for three long months. The man I had initially hated as a child had now become someone I had grown very close to. I helped my mother as much as I could, lifting Eric and helping to turn him over. My mother was beginning to look tired and worn out, and Eric was becoming weaker and weaker. He started screaming with pain. Mum was crying night and day she could see the love of her life slipping away. With all the medication he was taking, he was in and out of consciousness.

In the last few days Eric spent with us, he began seeing things in the room, on the ceiling. Mum just sat holding his hand, wiping his forehead and just generally being there for him. What was for sure was that Eric was never going to pass over without my mum being with him all the way. His pain got to a point where even medication could not help.

Mum asked me to sit with him while she went to the phone box to ring the doctor. When she got back he had started to drift in and out. The doctor came within the hour. He took one look at Eric and said, 'I'm sorry Mrs Graham, we've done all we can for him'.

Mum shouted, 'No! You've got to help him, he has suffered enough'.

Dr Smith said, 'This is strictly between us'. What he did that day was the most humane act I've ever witnessed. He injected Eric with what was obviously an overdose of morphine. Within seconds he was free of pain and on his long journey home. Needless to say, Mum was holding his hand throughout. She had never left that man's side, day or night for three months.

The next six months after Eric had gone were very hard for me, and more so for mum. She had just lost her world. I had lost someone who I had never thought could be a friend.

Eric's family were, to say the least, very difficult. His daughter Betty was so upset that Eric had ended his days in my mother's arms. She understandably thought his place was with her mother, just as I had thought my mother's place was with my father, and not with hers. I think these are the thoughts of young children, not adults. It's so easy to make judgements at that age. The truth is, you're just too young to understand.

I'm so glad mum found those four short years so happy. Betty appeared to be bitter for years after the death of her father, more with my mother rather than with me, but I think she knew in her heart that her dad was loved, cherished and adored by my mother. She couldn't have dreamed of a better place for him to end his days. My mother was an angel to Betty's dad. I really hope in Betty's heart she found forgiveness towards my mother, and realised her dad had died in peace. RIP Eric.

Mum was never to find true love again, even though not long after that she married my stepdad, Jack Rafter, a fantastic man, a great father to me and not just a stepdad. She was married to Jack for about 12 years. First he asked my mother if she would consider moving in with him at Shay Lane. She was a little unsure about this move because she was still grieving for Eric, so on the first occasion she turned him down. My god, Jack was disappointed. He went off with his tail between his legs. But later that year, mum agreed to move in with him, so I helped her pack her home up and move it to Shay Lane. She took months to settle, but eventually she did.

Now during all this upheaval, what was I doing? I was joining the Coldstream Guards.

CHAPTER 5

Almost a Guardsman

———❦———

When I initially went to enquire about joining the Guards, I spoke to a sergeant behind the desk in the Army Careers Office. He said 'Morning, can I help?' I replied, 'How do I join the French Foreign Legion?' He gasped and said 'Bloody hell lad, things must be bad in your life', then laughed. I asked, 'Is it that bad?'

He said 'Imagine crawling across glass on your bare belly'.

I said, 'OK, forget that idea. What do you recommend?'

That's when he said, 'A big lad like you wants to join the Coldstream Guards'. He sat me down and booked me in for a test and a medical. So off I went and broke the news to my mother and Jack. They were over the moon for me.

One week later I took the test and achieved 82 correct out of 100 questions. However, I would have got 100 out of 100 if I hadn't foolishly gone to a nightclub the night before. I passed the exam and the medical, to my surprise, but the medical part was to come back later and bite me firmly in the backside.

I put my notice in at Walton Colliery, and I always remember the overman Raymond saying, 'Don't come back for a job here, Kev'.

I said 'Not as I'll need it, but why Raymond?'

He said, 'This pit's closing'.

I stood and laughed in disbelief, because I had never in my 18 years heard of a pit closing. He shouted down the corridor as I walked off, 'Don't forget to bring your barnet back with you if you want the job back'. I carried on walking and laughed in disbelief.

My friend Lou Harrison was already serving in the light infantry, and he was my inspiration to join the Army. Lou was a larger than life character. He was a man mountain, standing six foot tall and built like a chest of drawers, and his heart was bigger than his chest. What a lovely guy. He was born and bred in Streethouse. We all attended different schools, but that doesn't mean we were all enemies. We would very often see one another when we visited each other's villages. During the 70s kids would accept you or make your life bloody hell. I never had any problems, and knowing Lou made life much easier.

Me and Lou were good friends. He made me feel welcome whenever our paths crossed. On one occasion Lou was going to Northern Ireland to serve during the Troubles. We were both in the Weavers Green pub at Crofton when he told me he was about to do this tour. I took my St Christopher off my neck and placed it around his neck. I said, 'Please take this with you Lou'. He started laughing and said 'Don't be silly Kev, it'll give the IRA something to shoot at'. He gave it back and I put it back around my neck. We had a great night, and when Lou was leaving we shook hands and hugged each other.

That was the last time I ever saw him. The day before his tour finished in Northern Ireland there was a car bomb alert. The light infantry and Lou attended and tried to get people away from the bomb. However it turned out to be a trap and a sniper shot Lou through the chest with an Armalite round. He was pronounced dead at the scene.

His mam and dad had gone to Spain on holiday the day before he was murdered by the IRA. They had left all his clothes laid out on his bed for him to change into when he arrived home, but he would never arrive home again. The best-looking lad in Streethouse and the most entertaining guy in Yorkshire. I was devastated when I heard the news through the grapevine.

He was given a military funeral and a headstone, but some IRA coward kicked over the headstone and broke it. I hope the person who carried out this disgusting action has died a very painful death, though even that will never make up for what he did to Lou.

I spoke to everyone about Lou's life and his friendship with me. I will never forget that fantastic young man. Lou, one day we will meet again. I feel sure the first thing I will see is that huge smile. God bless you.

About two weeks after the funeral I caught the high-speed train to London to join the Army. I had never been on a high-speed train, or to London, in my life. On the train I needed the toilet, but I didn't know how to open the carriage door. This really nice chap jumped up from his seat and pushed the little silver button on the door. The door opened and I felt a right plonker.

When I reached Kings Cross station I had to navigate my way through the Underground to the station I was due to be picked up from. I sat and waited for about fifteen minutes and got bored, so I walked over to the local pub and ordered a pint of beer, which looked like cold tea. Anyway this girl walked up to me at the bar and said 'Would you like a game of darts?' so I said yes. We started playing, and she started getting a little suggestive. I was just about to say 'sorry love, I think you've picked the wrong man today' when the Regimental Sergeant Major walked into the pub. He looked straight at me and said, 'Are you Kevin Graham?' I said yes. He shouted,

'Get your arse in that Land Rover outside'. So I grabbed my bag and jumped into the Land Rover. He marched out of the pub and got in the front of the vehicle and said, 'Do you want to go home with a cauliflower on the end of your cock, son?' No, I replied. He said, 'Guardsmen are gentlemen, not lowlife, so leave the lowlife alone.'

I replied, 'Yes I will'.

'That's yes I will SERGEANT MAJOR!'

From then on I watched my Ps & Qs.

When I arrived at the camp in Pirbright I was shown to my barracks, then taken to the Army stores. What an experience that was. I walked down a line of store staff standing behind a long counter, and they piled uniforms, boots and helmets into my arms and onto my head. Then I was off again to the barracks, where I had to put it all away in my locker. Then, to my astonishment, the Sergeant entered the room and said, 'Kevin, you're in barracks two weeks too early. Now do you want to go back home or wait here for the rest of the group to turn up?'

I thought, I'm not stopping here on my own and being told what to do for two weeks. Let's hit the underground and go back to Kings Cross. So I got my travel passes and went back home.

My mother was very surprised to see me, and Jack asked me a million questions. He had been with the RAF during WW2.

During the two weeks I was at home I ran up and down the railway banking to build on my fitness. The two weeks soon ticked away, and it was time to return to Pirbright. That was when I left reality and entered the lion's den of life. The first day back the drill sergeant sat all the new recruits down on the floor. He went on to say, 'Are you all aware of the bullying that's going on in the Guards?' He was referring to an article in the Sun newspaper. We all said yes sergeant, we had seen those reports. He said 'Don't worry, because it's twice as bad. When I say shit, you say where sir?'

We were all panicked, but from that point on I thought, if he says jump I'm going to say 'How high Sergeant?'

A lot of bullying went on in those days. We went on a cross-country run one day and the lad I was running alongside decided to jump a barbed wire fence to desert. I shouted to him, 'What are you doing?' He replied, 'Just keep running Kev, don't tell them.' So when we all returned we were counted in and obviously one was missing. They asked if anyone had witnessed this lad absconding and we all said no. The sergeant knew we were lying, so he made us all do 50 press-ups.

Three days later the lad was captured and brought back to camp. I saw him at the guardhouse. He was stripped to his underpants and made to run around the guardhouse. At each corner stood a guard with a baseball bat, and as the young lad ran past they hit him with the bat. They made him run until he fell down in pain from the beating. It was very distressing to see that young lad go through hell at the hands of our so-called tutors of warfare, but it taught me a lesson, and that lesson was, don't upset these guys, just do as you're told.

My training was going really well until one day I didn't open my eyes as quickly as the drill sergeant would have liked. That's my way of saying I had slept in. What a bloody mistake that was. He ran over to my bed and tipped me straight out of my lovely warm and comfortable bed. As you can imagine, I was in a mood, so I jumped up and put my fists up. He laughed and said, 'Bring it on son'. I suddenly realised what I was doing. I immediately lowered my fists and dropped my head and apologised. He said, 'If you show me disrespect again you will find yourself running and knocking press-ups out for two hours. Do I make myself clear?' I shouted, 'Yes sergeant'. He said, 'Get dressed on the double'. I thanked God for my let-off.

Later that week we were on the firing range. He shouted 'cease fire!' and I let one more round off. The sergeant ran down the line, and when he got to me he kicked me straight in the ribs, and shouted, 'You stupid bastard, that round could have shot a guardsman in a war zone'. Again I had to apologise. And again God was on my side.

But a much bigger blow was to come. Later that week I was called to the CO's office, and he asked me about the heart problems I had had as a child. I told him I had been born with a heart murmur. He asked why I had never mentioned this at my initial medical. I replied 'I didn't think it was relevant sir'. He said, 'You must go straight from my office to see the MO and get this condition checked out'. So I marched over to the MO's office and stripped down to my waist. He examined me and said, 'This murmur is still present and very evident. I'm afraid I will have to medically discharge you'.

I said 'Sir, there's no need for that, I feel fine'.

He said 'Mr Graham, don't answer back. You will be discharged on grounds of ill health'. So I had to go back to my barracks, change into my civilian clothes and report to the CO again. He said, 'Once more, you should have made us aware of this condition. However, during the time you have been with us you have been extremely good and I'm sorry to lose you'. He then passed me my discharge papers and my rail passes.

I was in tears when I left his office. I had achieved so much getting into the guards and making new friends. As I walked out of the camp for the last time I turned and took a long look. I had really wanted this to be part of my youth. That moment in time was among the most hurtful I have ever felt.

I turned and carried on walking to the bus stop and I caught the bus back to the local railway station. My heart had sunk into my stomach, and I felt sick. When I arrived at the station I felt my whole life had been turned upside down. As I sat on the station bench I spotted a bunch of paras going home on leave, and I was green with envy. I climbed on board the train thinking life had just deserted me. When I arrived at King's Cross Station I passed so many down-and-outs it was unbelievable, all constantly begging. I had never seen begging on this scale before. My first thought was that this was my destiny.

When I reached home my mother and stepdad were astonished to see me. When I explained what had happened they were both so sympathetic towards me, which made my return a lot easier. That night I dropped into bed and slept like an old sheepdog that had been working the dales all day. Sleep was something I hadn't had a great deal of during the short time when I had been a soldier in the great regiment of the Coldstream Guards.

CHAPTER 6

The family way

A few days later Sheena, the girl who had forced my hand to join the Guards in the first place, suddenly revealed she was pregnant. This was a massive shock. Not only had I lost my career in the British Army, I was now faced with this revelation. But we met and talked, and finally our relationship blossomed and developed into marriage. I had been seeing this girl since I was at secondary school. I should have spotted the telltale signs that it was not going to be a long-term relationship.

Regardless of that, we had two lovely girls, Sharn Louise and Zara Elizabeth. However our two wonderful kids didn't seal the marriage. Sheena never showed me or the kids any affection. If I ever took her out for a social drink, I never returned home with her, because she would throw herself at other men once I'd gone home in a mood.

Finally she did something to make me look like a mouse, not a man. We had gone to a club in Wakefield with some friends, Mick and Ann Jackson, a great couple. That night was to prove to be the last showing up she would put me through. On arrival I went to the bar for drinks with Mick, and she and Ann went to the dance floor, so Mick and I went down there and told them 'Your drinks are over here'. They said 'Yes, we're just having a dance.' With that I walked back to Mick, who was watching the drinks and the handbags.

Three hours later they still hadn't returned. I was full of hell by this time, so I made my way onto the dance floor. When I got there they were both with a gang of lads who quite obviously thought they had pulled two girls. I shouted 'Right, that's the last time you show me up'. At that point one of the lads said, 'Who do you think you're shouting at?' I said 'Don't get cocky with me mate'.

He made a move towards me and I pushed him backwards, and before I knew where I was the bouncer had thrown me out of the club. Sheena followed me, and so did Mick and Ann. We got into a taxi without speaking. Suddenly she said, 'Are we ok?' I said, 'If there was a solicitor's open now I would divorce you'. I then turned round and never spoke all the way home.

Once I got home I told her mother what she had been like and slept on the sofa. The next morning I went to ask Jack and my mother if I could return home, and they both said 'Yes love'. So I went back with Jack and we removed all my clothes.

This was to be one of the lowest times in my life. The pain I felt leaving those two little girls behind was devastating. I had no one to turn to other than my sister during those dark days – she helped me through it. But one night I decided I wanted to see my girls, so I went to the house of horror, but I found a man there, in the house I had worked for. My blood was boiling, and I called her all the names under the sun. She said 'I've moved on,' and slammed the door in my face. I was raging. I went to the house of a friend who lived about 20 yards away. I knew he had a shotgun and by this time I had had enough. My plan was to steal this shotgun from his house and murder the two bastards who were getting pleasure out of making my life hell, but unfortunately, or fortunately, whichever way you look at this situation, my friend was not in. Otherwise it would have been the final disaster.

I was at my lowest ebb that night. I returned to my mum's in tears and went to my cold, quiet bedroom. Mum insisted that I should ring the doctor the next day and explain how I felt, so the next morning I rang the doctor's surgery and explained my situation. They insisted I should see Dr Vaughan that very morning. When I attended the appointment, Dr Vaughan was visibly upset for me. He gave me some tablets and said, 'You must start these straight away'.

When I went home I took my tablets. I felt so dizzy and tired it was unbelievable. After that all I did was sleep. My mother was so concerned about me that she rang Dr Vaughan and told him I was sleeping all the time and I never left my little bedroom. He said, 'Don't worry, Kevin will recover from this'.

My mother wasn't convinced. She watched me like a hawk for the next month. Then finally I decided I could not live like that anymore, so I went to the toilet and tipped the tablets down the toilet.

Mother shouted, 'Kevin, what are you doing?' I replied, 'I'm getting shut of this shocking life'. She was taken by surprise by what I did. However, I had to start looking forward and not back.

From that day my life changed. My brothers never bothered about my health or my mother's concerns, they just went about their lives. The only sibling who cared was my sister Christine. She was always there for me. In fact one day she asked if I would like my hair cutting, as she had invited a young mobile hairdresser to call round, so I said yes, I could do with a trim.

The next day I went to my sister's. The young hairdresser, whose name was Paula, was already doing Christine's hair, and a soon as I saw her I was head over heels in love. She was the most beautiful girl I had ever seen. I looked into her gorgeous blue eyes and saw youth, sincerity and love. All this just blew me away, and I knew I just had to meet her and take her out. I tried so hard to be the Kev who had loved life before a woman had shattered it. I began to make her laugh and feel comfortable around me. Then I thought, this girl I cannot let go, so I plucked up the courage to ask her out. To my surprise, she agreed to go for a drink.

Now I had to think of somewhere nice to take her. She seemed a bit classy for Crofton Club. Then it came to me: the Windmill. This was a quiet pub on the fringes of Crofton.

When the night came, Paula picked me up from mum's. The first thing she said was, 'Where are we going then?' so I piped up, 'The Windmill on Doncaster Road'.

When we arrived at the pub she looked a little disappointed, and she certainly was when we went in. In true Kev style I fronted it out, but eventually I had to concede, so I said, 'Shall we go to the Sharlston Hotel?' and she jumped at the chance.

That night was the best night I'd had in years – I never wanted it to end – but of course, end it did. Paula dropped me back at my mum's. Then the dreaded first kiss. I had really wanted to kiss her all night, but I didn't want to appear to be pushy. We kissed in her little 1972 VW Herbie. Life had just started again for Kev Graham.

At that period in my life I was working as a crematorium attendant. Paula found this fascinating, and she would drive to the crematorium to pick me up after work. She would always come inside and ask about a thousand questions. I always looked forward to see her lovely little face, but the questions were as if I was sitting in the TV Mastermind seat. Bless her, her intentions were good, and over the coming weeks and months she saved me and my sorry little life from disaster. Without Paula I know to this day that my life would have spiralled out of control. The affection, love and laughter she brought back into my world was amazing. I will never be able to thank her enough, in this life or the next.

Needless to say, my love for this amazing girl was soon put to the test. Sheena began blackmailing me with my two children, saying they were suffering with my absence and crying endlessly at night. I had no love left for that woman, but my heart was being ripped out worrying about my two lovely little girls, so once again I made a decision to return to the kids.

To tell Paula about my intentions was soul destroying. She asked me to reconsider; she was so upset. But I could only picture those girls crying themselves to sleep on a night, so with great regret I returned to the home that I'd left in pieces. I kissed and hugged the kids, but when Sheena approached me I felt no attraction towards her.

This was a very embarrassing moment. She looked down at the floor and said, 'Thank you for coming back home. Maybe your feelings will return'.

I just knew they would never return. I lasted two weeks without Paula, and I couldn't bear it any longer. On many occasions at work I would ring her and chat and laugh along with her. I would sing, 'I'm all out of love' to her. This record reminded so much of her and the massive mistake I had made returning to the house where I felt no love.

I never unpacked the suitcase Paula had packed for me to return to the kids. After two weeks I told Sheena, 'I can't stay here any longer. I feel no love for you, although I love those girls with every drop of love I possess in my body. However, my life is waiting to start again. There's only one person who makes me feel like she loves me and wants me for me, and that person is Paula.' Then I picked up the phone and rang my stepdad Jack to pick me up.

My mother thought the baby Sheena was now carrying was mine, so as you can imagine she was rather upset that I had decided to return to her back bedroom. But that wasn't the truth; I had hidden the real truth from my mother, because I knew if my return to the kids was to work out then my mother had to think the new baby was mine. When I told her the truth she changed completely and really welcomed me back home. She couldn't believe I had lied to protect the kids, but I had. Yet another mistake to add to the rest.

But before all this discussion took place, when Jack pulled up outside to collect me I kissed the girls and once again I left in pieces. When I'd put my clothes in the car I returned home on my motorbike. When I arrived, to my surprise Paula was standing in my mother's kitchen. I was so happy to see her that I yanked my helmet off to hug and kiss her. However I had forgotten that during the last two weeks I'd grown a beard. Her eyes nearly fell out. But needless to say she kissed and hugged me, and that's what I needed. Her reassurance meant everything to me. We picked up the pieces once again and moved on. She breathed life back into my dead body. I knew there was only one love in my life, and I was determined not to lose her again.

We loved, laughed and shared so many enjoyable moments together. One such moment was when we decided to go to Whitby with my mother and stepdad Jack, and my mother packed a picnic in Jack's shining Datsun. We embarked on a wonderful day out.

We stopped at Thornton-le-Dale on the way to Whitby. My mother loved this beautiful scenic place, and she got her little table out of the boot of the car along with two chairs. Then the picnic – mother had made a beef joint and carved it up before leaving home to make the sandwiches. They were second to none.

Paula and I tucked into the picnic and then I decided to capture the moment on film. After we filled up on beef and various sweet stuffs we pushed on to Whitby. We all took in the views, the lovely smells of the sea, and let's not forget the fish & chips. After eating half a cow on fresh bread, we still managed to enjoy fish & chips on the sea front.

That day out will always be a happy memory. It was one of those days you wish would never end. Many, many times I have wished I could turn the clock back to that lovely stress-free day.

But we had many more enjoyable and memorable days like that one, and we started to fall more and more in love with each other. We felt so happy that we decided to take our relationship to another level. After three years of enjoying each other's company, we decided to make it permanent and get married. So on January 18th 1986, Kev and Paula became one.

We had a little terraced house, number 4 Garden Row, Crofton. We paid £10,500 for that little love shack, with the help of a big mortgage. Paula was a very successful hairdresser and I had a good job at the crematorium, so in reality we had no problems paying the mortgage, but that never stopped us worrying about it.

Then we decided we needed a little friend sharing in that love with us. I mean a little dog, not a little human. So we searched the papers and asked people we knew, and finally we found a beautiful little Staffordshire bull terrier. He and his six siblings were for sale in Leeds, so we made an appointment and went to see them. The one we chose was a right little tearaway – he was fighting with his mother and ragging plants around the house. We thought, he's full of spirit, he's the one for us, so we bought him and took him home.

We settled him down in front of the fire and crept up to bed. At the bottom of the stairs we had a sliding door which we thought he would never breach, but he smashed straight through it and ran upstairs to me and Paula. We were in rapturous laughter over the next eighteen months, and our little friend was a fantastic addition to our home. We named him Staff. He loved kids and people and adored me and Paula. But there always has to be a but... he hated other dogs, so he had to be kept on a leash. The dog down the street would constantly have a go at Staff. It was as if it knew he was always on a lease and couldn't hurt him, so he would bark and snarl as he passed.

Then one day I opened the car door directly outside our back doorstep, opened the house door and shouted for Staff to jump into the car. As he strolled out of the house, the loudmouth dog from down the street was passing. Staff spotted him and flew in his direction. I tried to grab his collar, but he body-swerved me and grabbed the dog by its neck. Then he threw the dog into the air and was waiting for it to land to give the killer bite to its throat. Luckily I grabbed his collar and spared that loud-mouthed dog a sudden death.

We had so many good times with that fantastic bull terrier, but Paradise can't last for ever. One day Paula and I attended a barbecue at her mother's house. We took Staff with us, and as it was a red-hot day he lay in the house to keep cool. Unfortunately my wife's uncle's little girl, Louise. wouldn't stop pestering Staffy, and he snapped at her a couple of times.

I jumped up on both occasions and said 'Louise, leave him alone love, he's fed up now'.

Then out of the blue we heard a commotion. I ran into the house and saw Louise crying, and her face was bleeding. Obviously Staffy had attacked her because of the incessant pestering. Once her mother and father saw her they said they wanted Staffy put to sleep. We were in pieces. Our little dog didn't deserve that. However, if they had taken us to court for that incident, the court would have insisted we had him destroyed, even though it was not his fault.

So reluctantly we took the decision to end Staffy's life, thanks to my wife's unsympathetic family. We didn't take him straight away – we tried to do everything to save him, but we couldn't.

I took him to the local vet and explained what had happened. He was reluctant to put him to sleep, but under the circumstances he had to. He cut the hair on his paw to expose the poor little dog's vein and said to me, 'Are you ready?' I said yes. By this time tears were rolling down my cheeks. Staffy looked at me so sadly. The needle was put into the vein and the vet administered the injection. Staffy fell into my arms. He was so warm and smelt lovely. The veterinary staff left me with his beautiful body for a few minutes. I was heartbroken. I will never forget that dog, or forgive the ones who condemned him to his untimely death.

On a lighter note, during our time living at Garden Row we had fantastic neighbours. The first ones that spring to mind were Ian and Caroline Henderson, who lived at No 3. They had a beautiful little boy called Ian, and these guys were dream neighbours. Ian was a roofer by trade and a very good one. Both of us were always looking for ways to make extra cash. He was the tradesman, and I was the mouthpiece that drummed up work.

I remember once we were working on a roof in the opposite street to ours, Hope Terrace. We were both getting really hungry, so Ian climbed down our ladder to ask his wife Caroline to make us both a bacon sandwich. At this point I was looking forward to this sandwich like a bear that hasn't eaten all winter. Ian climbed back up the ladder and as he reached the top run he said, 'The sandwich is being cooked as we speak' and licked his lips. We carried on working, and after about thirty minutes I said to Ian, 'Is there a problem with the sandwich?' He frowned and said, 'that bloody woman'. He then went down the ladder again. He had been gone about five minutes and I was becoming really hungry and cold, so I went down too.

Once I got to the bottom I walked over to Ian's house and asked him what had happened to the sandwich. Caroline had put the bacon under the grill and turned the gas to the lowest flame. She looked at me and said, 'I didn't want to burn it Kev'. I replied, 'Caz, have you paid the bloody gas bill or what? I've never seen anybody turn the gas so low to cook something'.

Needless to say I took over the cooking duties, and soon after me and Ian were eating the most needed sandwich in my working career. The sandwiches gave us a laugh and made a break in our morning of work.

Many nights out preceded this job and many more jobs preceded those nights out. We all bonded together and enjoyed each other's company. Little Ian would toddle into our house sucking his dummy. Our dog Staffy would pinch the dummy out of Ian's mouth and run around the house with it. Ian would giggle and laugh uncontrollably. I would chase the dog to retrieve the dummy and little Ian would fall to the floor giggling. After a great chase I would corner Staff and pinch the dummy off him, then wash it and return it to its owner. This entertainment happened regularly.

Then suddenly little Ian became unwell. We all thought it was just an ordinary virus, but it was much more than that. His body started to deteriorate and within two months he had died. We were all devastated, and Ian and Caroline were in pieces.

I remember going to the chapel of rest to pay our respects to little Ian. We were shown to a little room as we entered the room and straight away the little coffin was visible. As we got closer I could see little Ian laid inside the little white coffin dressed in a silk blue and white sailor suit. Paula and I were in tears, Ian was sobbing and Caroline sat holding little Ian's hand and crying uncontrollably. After about 10 minutes Caroline said to me, 'Kevin, little Ian's hand is warm, do you think he's coming round?' I sobbed and said 'Caroline, no love, it's your hand that's warming his'.

After this heart-wrenching visit to pay our last respects to little Ian, Paula and I tried to help these two heartbroken people. We drummed up support for a fund-raising night in our local pub, the Royal Oak. I offered my services free of charge to dig little Ian's grave. We didn't know how to ease the stress and anxiety both Ian and Caroline were going through, but we did everything in our power to help.

The day of the funeral was one of the saddest I have ever experienced. To see a child's coffin lowered into a grave you yourself have dug is soul-destroying. I could not pick up a shovel and start throwing soil on that little lad, so I employed a friend to fill the grave in after the service. We went to a funeral tea afterwards and tried so hard to rise a smile, but we all tried to lighten the spirts of Ian and Caroline and I hope we did. We will never forget that little lad.

On a lighter note, after 18 months in the little love nest next door to Ian and Caroline on Garden Row, I went to the club for a couple of drinks. Alan Gardener approached me and asked if I would consider selling our house to him.

Well, I was gobsmacked. Then I thought of pound notes. 'Yes,' I replied, 'give me £14,500 and it's yours.' Straight away he shook my hand and said, 'I'll bring Debbie round tomorrow. If she's happy you've got a deal.'

Now at this point I've got to go home and tell Paula I had just sold our little love nest without even thinking where we were going to live. I felt like a disabled gladiator going into the arena with a broken sword. I knew Paula would go mad.

I went home and broke the news, and it went down like a pork chop in a synagogue. She said, 'Are you mad? Where are we going?'

Now that I hadn't thought about. I've always been a great believer in fate and the idea that life is mapped out for each and everyone of us. So I was rather hoping this map was about to find me a house.

Sure thing, the very next day a friend told me about a couple on Farnham Way who were splitting up. That was my cue to go round and knock on the door. I knew the lady who was selling it as I'd gone to school with her. I started bartering on the price, and she eventually agreed on £18,500. We loved the house – it was a great step up for us, although then we started worrying about meeting the mortgage payments.

Within two months we were ready to say goodbye to our first little house and a big hello to our new adventure on Farnham Way. Paula and I were on holiday when the contracts were exchanged. Luckily for us our parents moved us in, so when we returned from holiday we just had to put our cases away. Bonus!

We enjoyed our time in that house, and we would scheme how to make extra money. I would be out gravedigging while Paula would be cleaning washers, cookers and anything else she could get her hands on. Life was so eventful then – you just never knew what was going to happen next.

Come the weekend we would be counting our extra cash and on occasion we would be in the club bobbing a couple of pots off. One night we had both been tripping the light fantastic at the club. It was great at the time, but when we got back home we decided to fall out over something ridiculous, and after a bickering match Paula decided to kick through the glass in the front door. The argument fizzled out, she went to bed and I was left with the repair. As I was on my hands and knees putting a new pane of glass in, our next door neighbour came home. He took one look at what I was doing and said 'I see it's been a good night Kev'. I laughed and said 'Cheers, Billy'.

As for Billy and his wife Julie, one of their most memorable arguments was another Saturday night when Billy had been out on the beer. He came home about midnight with a wobble on. He went straight to bed but around 2 am Julie woke both me and Paula up, shouting at Billy, 'You've just pissed in my knicker drawer!' The next morning there must have been thirty pairs of knickers on the washing line. So we all had our problems when we were young.

The area and the house was great, but as a young couple you never settle and always want to cut out a wonderful house for each other. Soon Paula and I started to get itchy feet for an even bigger house, because by now our little angel had arrived. Hannah Victoria Graham was born on February 11 1990. This little girl had made our marriage complete, but we still needed a bigger house.

The next day I put the house up for sale, telling Paula, 'Don't worry, no one will buy it straight away. We'll have time to look around this time'.

Yes, you guessed it. The same day the house went up for sale, a guy turned up and bought it. He said 'I want to move in as soon as possible'. At that point I felt Paula's big blue eyes burning into me, but a sale is a sale, so in true Kev form I said 'Fine, we want to be out asap'. In reality of course, we had nowhere to go.

It looked like it was down to that thing fate again. Yes, you know what I'm about to say. A friend told me about an old lady in Cherry Tree Crescent, Walton, who had recently died and her house was empty, so I was in there like a ferret down a pipe. The next day I was down there making enquiries. The next-door neighbour was a lovely woman called Charlotte. She told me the house was tired, but not beyond repair. With that in mind I contacted the estate agents and made a silly offer of £40,000. I was shocked when they agreed.

Once we got the keys we both understood what Charlotte meant about 'a little tired'. The walls were covered in eight by four wood sheets that didn't match. The fire and fireplace looked like they had been supplied by Steptoe and Son. The kitchen looked like something off the Clampetts in the Beverley Hillbillies. All in all it was a typical Kev buy. Oops!

My first real encounter with the neighbours was on the day we moved in, December 23 1992. I knocked on the door to be greeted by Charlotte. I asked, 'Do you have a little sugar I could borrow?' Charlotte said 'Yes, pop in love'. So without further ado I walked in. On looking round I couldn't see a Christmas tree, so I said, 'You're late putting the Christmas tree up'.

Charlotte replied 'No love, we're Jehovah's Witnesses'.

I said straight out, 'What, all of you?' She replied 'Yes, all the lot'. I could have died and gone straight to hell. But please make sure you don't do what I have always done and judge a book by its cover, because as the weeks and months went on, the family of 'Jovies' next door became fantastic friends. Paula and I had nine beautiful years at that house, and Charlotte and Allan never once in those nine years mentioned religion.

However the other next-door neighbour, Scotch Charlie, was hated by half the village, although he was revered by the other half. We nearly came to blows on several occasions. One of these occasions was over an aerial wire that was flapping and tapping on my window. This wire was running down my side of our semi-detached building. However, Charlie thinks differently. According to him, this part of my house belonged to him. So the aerial men start to clip the loose wire down to my house. Out comes Charlie, shouting 'What the fucking hell are you doing, Kevin?'

So I replied, 'These guys are clipping the wire down.'

Charlie said, 'Well I'll tell you this, See this wire? I'll pull the fucking thing off the wall when these guys go.'

I said, 'You pull that off and I'll pull your fucking head off'. Then, to my surprise, Paula said, 'Kev, get me that bloody jigsaw, I'll cut this wood panel in half.'

Charlie looked at Paula, and if looks could kill she would have been stone dead. He retreated back into his house, muttering and swearing.

The next day Charlie called me inside and apologised. He didn't speak to Paula for four years, but I think he became a better person for the falling out. He often smiled and laughed like a normal person.

The neighbours on the other side of Charlie were Steve and Sharon Carswell, and they had two great little lads, Matthew and Thomas. Matthew was always the kid with the red number 11 running down his face because he had a constant problem with his nose. Thomas was a thumb sucker, not a chatterbox like his brother. That lad would ask about a thousand questions a day and never leave me alone. The best talent he had was being able to identify car keys just by looking at them, and he was no more than three years old. I was amazed at his ability to identify car keys.

This family had been dealing with Charlie for years. On one occasion Steve, Sharon and the kids went to Morocco for two weeks' holiday. On their return Charlie had put a fence up between their two houses. Steve came round to my house and said, 'Have you seen what Charlie has built between our houses?' I said no, and he invited me to come and look. 'It's the bloody Berlin Wall', he said.

I walked round and took a look. 'That fence is huge, Steve,' I said.

'I'm going to burn that bastard down,' he told me. I calmed him down and said 'Steve, there's a silver lining in every cloud'. He looked at me and said, 'What do you mean?'

I said, 'That fence is eight foot tall, that means you don't have to look at Charlie's miserable face anymore'.

He said 'Yes, that's true, I'm not burning it, I'm going to paint it.' We both stood laughing.

When I walked back home, the Chambers family across the road, Brian and Sue with their three daughters, were playing out on the street. As Brian and I were talking his youngest daughter, Megan, decided to bend down and shit at the top of my drive, so I drew Brian's attention to what had just happened. He said, 'Bloody hell, have you got a tissue on you Kev?'

I said 'A tissue Brian? I think you need a sheet out of the Wakefield Express'. What a bloody pile that was for a little girl of three.

The street and the close community were a great place to live and be among, but after nine years of living on Cherry Tree Crescent, we decided it was time to move on. The house went for sale on the Monday and by Friday it was sold, so once again we had to pull a house quickly out of the bag.

I took Hannah to school one day and decided to drive through Ashdene. As I entered Ashdene I looked up Church Way, and there it was, my saviour: no. 5 Church Way, a beautiful 2-bedroom bungalow. I returned home and said to Paula, 'Come on, you need to see this'.

Off we went, and as soon as she looked at the bungalow she loved it. I rang Richard Kendal, the estate agent, and they sent a representative down there straight away. He came and we said SOLD.

Within a month we had moved in. The house, the neighbours and the area were fantastic.

Let the stress begin.

Cuddling my nephew Bryan.

The start of my money-making years.

My dad and his pitmates. RIP Dad.

Me and the lads waiting to grab an onion.

My new life with my lovely wife Paula begins, 1986.

Teddy bears' picnic – Mam, Jack, Paula and me.

My first school.

Proudest moment of my schooldays – Yorkshire cup winners.

Freddy & Madge Palmers' fish shop. Our soup kitchen.

The man who could fall out in an empty house. Steve Totty's Dad, a fantastic role model

Great mate Zoot with lifelong friends Trev and Angie Chalkley.

Alf Hill's, the Lump's salvation.

Trev reminisces about his past life in the beloved pits of Yorkshire.

Where life began for Crofton lads – streets of dreams.

Johnny and me having a day to remember – he's given me a life to remember.

The calm before the storm.

The Third Reich who taught me in the junior school.

Sweet little Iain Henderson, R.I.P.

The wife, holding on to her man.

She was, and is, so lovely. In Vegas.

Hannah trying to hide her pocket money.

Staffy, the dog that lives on in my heart.

Mother Big Reen and Auntie Glad. Two women this world will never replace – RIP.

Two of my best Christmas gifts – Max and Minnie.

My lifetime friend Steve Totty (spot), nine years a Marine.

My great mate Dave Endersby and sister Carol.

Three beautiful lives that changed mine.

My eldest daughter Sharn and and her three children, my grandkids.

Rocking around the Christmas tree – Max and Minnie. .

With my youngest daughter Hannah

Once we stood tall as a family, but never again.

The start of my prison service and the worst chapter of my life

If the cap fits...

Hannah, Max and Minnie - three little heartbeats.

Remembrance of first Holy Communion

John Rafton received first Holy
Communion on April 17ᵗ 1924 in the Church of
The Sacred Heart Hemsworth

My stepfather Jack Rafter gave his life to the Catholic Church. Now I hope Jesus is giving him a special life in return. RIP Jack.

The man I am now leaning on - the man I will become. One thing that will never change – I'm still made of iron.

CHAPTER 7

Prison officer

⸻◇⸻

By now my pub career was coming to an end and my prison service career was about to start.

I was pencilled in to start at HMP Brixton, London, but at the eleventh hour HMP & YOI Newhall stepped in and asked me if i would like to work there instead.

Now Brixton is 300 miles away and Newhall was 7 miles away, so it's a no-brainer, or that's what you would think. I had good and bad times within this establishment.

Prisons are really weird places, as I'm sure you can imagine.

Firstly looking at the good times. My youngest daughter Hannah had started to be a little tearaway, so when she was 14 years old I asked the security governor if I could give her a tour of the prison so she could see what the consequences of bad behaviour would be. He agreed. Before I brought Hannah I spoke to some prisoners who were very nasty pieces of work and were doing time for crimes that are unrepeatable. They agreed to help me convince her that she should listen to her dad and stop being a pain in the arse.

So I brought Hannah to the prison. At that time all prisoners were locked away for staff to take lunch, however skeleton staff were left on wings to make sure all inmates were okay and suicide risks were monitored.

Hannah and I went to E wing, where 100 inmates were kept. First we passed through the hospital wing, which may sound like it would be full of sick people, but in fact it was for inmates with mental health problems, the most demanding people in the system.

So I called to see one of the most troubled inmates on that wing. She looked at Hannah and said in a nasty voice, 'you must listen to your dad, otherwise you'll get a cell in this madhouse'. Hannah stood looking at the woman, but she didn't reply, so the woman shouted, 'Did you fucking hear me bitch?'

Hannah squeezed my hand – she was scared. I had to tell the inmate, 'There's no need to swear. I believe Hannah understands, don't you Hannah?'

Hannah just nodded. I thanked the woman and closed the inspection hole. We then walked across to E wing. I knew at this point that Hannah was really scared. When we reached E wing she once again grabbed my hand and said 'Dad, don't leave me'.

'No love I won't leave you, but remember I don't want you to ever leave me, so take notice of what these people are telling you.'

'I will,' she replied.

I took over from the officers, who were chomping at the bit to go for lunch. I sat at the desk and started to sort out the prisoners' mail. Once I had sorted it out, Hannah said, 'Does a postman come now Dad?'

I said 'No, you're the postman love. So start at that cell and carry on going round the cells looking at the numbers on the envelopes and the doors'.

With that she set off on her new duties. As she posted the letters through the gaps in the door and the surrounds, inmates were snatching the letters and saying 'who are you?' Hannah replied, 'I'm Mr Graham's daughter'. They were shouting, 'this is Mr Graham's naughty little girl'.

Hannah was getting so nervous. I had to go on the landing and tell the inmates my daughter was helping out. They then became very warm towards her. Hannah felt protected by me and by one hundred locked steel doors.

I took her to see a very violent inmate. This woman had agreed to see her and show her how violent inmates could become. So I introduced Hannah to the inmate through the inspection hole. She went straight into a rage and said to Hannah, 'You don't know how lucky you are. Today you will go home with your dad. I'll be locked up in this cell until I'm allowed out. I don't have a mother or a dad like you. So unless you are off your fucking head, grow up quickly and don't fuck up the best dad you will ever meet. Are you with me, girl?'

Hannah once again nodded in agreement.

I said thank you to the inmate and closed the inspection hole and went back to the office. First question to Hannah was, 'Have you learnt anything today?'

She said 'Dad, I will never be stupid again and I certainly don't want a cell here or anywhere'.

Officers started to return to the wing after lunch. They all started to chat to me and Hannah. Now that was really nice of them, but when we started to leave the wing the rest of the prison started to unlock. Hannah should have been through the outer gates of the prison before movement of prisoners took place, but with us chatting, things didn't go to plan. Hannah was about to be bombarded by 400 inmates walking to work within the prison grounds. As soon as they saw her they ran towards us asking her for her name and admiring her gold jewellery. They even stroked her hair.

Hannah froze like an iced-over pond waiting for a huge brick being thrown into it. I had to be very forthright with the inmates and send them to work. It's difficult when you're alone with a 14-year-old girl, but out of respect for me and Hannah they all moved on and shouted 'bye, Hannah'.

When we returned home Hannah told her mum that she had been really scared and she would never do any stupid things again.

I have to say HMP and its inmates really did help on that occasion, as Hannah did very little wrong after that visit. But there was a cinder path waiting for me within the service. I was to find out later – not until seven years later – that in becoming a prison officer I had probably made one of the biggest mistakes of my life. There could only be one disaster that was bigger and more regrettable in my life, and that was failing to get into the Coldstream Guards – although that wasn't my fault.

During my time with HMP I met some strange people and some wonderful ones. Women prisoners were the most devious. They would smile at you, then try to attack you when you were not looking, physically and verbally. 90% of them were just doing their time and keeping their heads down. It was the 10% that were just looking for trouble and conflict that ruined careers. I encountered this 10% myself, and ultimately paid a heavy price. But not everything within the women's estate was all doom and gloom. The laughs I had while working within those walls were unbelievable.

One great story I must share with you was regarding a women who in all honesty should not have been in the normal prison community. She should have been on the health care unit, because of her mental health problems. One dinner time I was rotated to look after E wing and was sitting alone in the office sorting the inmates' mail out. As you can imagine, it was quite hectic for that hour. Wing officers were having lunch and relaxing while good old Kev was running around like a crazy man. Then out of the blue, a buzzer light came on. I looked for the light on the wing, and it was at the other end, so reluctantly I walked down to the cell. Once I arrived I turned off the buzzer and opened the inspection flap on the door. The woman I observed was well known to me because she had spent most of her prison term on the health care, where I was a regular officer.

As soon as she clocked my face, she smiled and said, 'Thank god it's you, Mr Graham'.

I asked why and she said, 'It's my own fault. I'm really sorry I slept with the window open last night.'

Rather irritated, I said 'Pat, what the hell is this all about?'

'A rat came through the open window and I must have slept with my mouth wide open, because it found its way into my stomach. So if you've got a knife handy I'll cut my stomach open and get the bloody thing out.'

I stood in amazement. I didn't know whether to laugh or call for back up. Anyway. whether I was right or wrong I said, 'Pat, there's no rat in your stomach'.

She said 'Look' and lifted her shirt up, showing me her stomach. She said, 'Can't you see the bastard running around my stomach?' I kept a straight face and said, 'Look Pat, I can't see anything. But after dinner I will report this incident to wing staff and they will deal with you.'

'OK' she said, 'but can't I just have a knife and save you the trouble of bothering staff?'

'No Pat, please try and have a sleep.'

With that the inmates either side of Pat shouted, 'Just give her that bleeding knife Mr Graham, then we can get some sleep.'

Obviously I told the two inmates to stop shouting. Then lo and behold, Pat said, 'You see, they think it's right I should have the knife'.

'Pat, there's no knife. Please lie on your bed and try to sleep with your mouth open. Maybe the rat will be ready to go and take a look around outside.'

Pat said, 'Yes, I knew you would have the answer, thank you Mr Graham'.

As I walked back to my office I was laughing so hard. Another inmate who had been listening to the wacky conversation said quietly through her door, 'You're full of shit, Mr Graham'. I replied 'Yes, but putting a stop to that ridiculous conversation gives me time to deliver your post.'

As usual with me, they were all saying, 'You've got a answer for everything'. I just laughed and pressed on to the office.

The story I'll share with you next is far from funny. It's chilling. The inmate in question was the most dangerous woman in the prison system. Her name will have to be kept private for obvious reasons, so we will refer to her as Miss A.

The first time I met Miss A was on the hospital wing. As I looked on the cell cameras all I could see in her cell was a big ball of blankets on the bed. Obviously she was under there somewhere. I spoke to the night officer and asked, 'Who's in that cell?'

She took a sharp intake of breath and said, 'Please be careful, she is one evil bitch. She will buzz you every half hour for you to drop her inspection hatch on her cell door for you to light her cig. This is what's been agreed by the governor. When she buzzes, keep your hands and arms well back. She may try to grab you through the hatch. She's really aggressive.'

So with that unnerving handover the officer left the wing, leaving the most dangerous female inmate with me. What a smashing day this was going to be.

It wasn't long before it was time to meet Miss A. Her buzzer rang out in the office. I turned off the buzzer and asked other staff to watch my back on the CCTV unit. They agreed, so off I nervously went. As I approached the cell I could hear Miss A coughing. I opened the inspection flap on her cell door, and as I dropped the flap she was standing with her face nearly touching the door. Her eyes were big and blue with red veins all over the whites.

Her first words to me were 'Who are you?' At this point the hair on the back of my neck was standing to attention. She was so intimidating it's hard to explain in words how I was engulfed in fear and panic, wondering how best to deal with this seriously disturbed individual.

'Mr Graham,' I said.

She just looked at me, analysing me. At that point she said in a deep and scary voice, 'Can I have a light for my cig?'

I produced the lighter that I carried around with me – a useful bit of equipment in the prison system. She asked if I smoked. I said in a light-hearted way, 'No, I carry it in case any good-looking girl needs a light for her cigarette'.

She looked straight into my eyes and said. 'You're a nice officer, I think I may like you'. Then she turned around and walked to her bed.

As I was closing the flap I said, 'It's nice to be liked'.

'For now,' I heard her say quietly. A statement like that plays with your mind. Does she like me, or is she thinking of attacking me? With this kind of inmate you could never be sure.

That first day working with Miss A was very intense, very stressful and most of all very much an eye-opener concerning psychological problems that another human being is suffering from and carrying around within themselves. Over the following week psychologists' reports and risk assessments were carried out on Miss A. The psychology report was unbelievable. It was hard to imagine a human being behaving as Miss A had whilst living amongst a normal population and during the long spells she had spent in various prison establishments.

We had received Miss A from Broadmoor Hospital, so I think most people would understand what kind of inmate I was dealing with. And over the coming weeks, months and years it really was my baby. In my own words and memories, I will endeavour to take you on that memorable time in my career.

Over the next few months, Miss A began to put great trust in me as an officer and a person. On lots of occasions I would be called for, wherever I was working within the prison – 'Get to the seg ASAP, Miss A is kicking off big style'. She had requested me, otherwise she was threatening to cut her breast off with a bone she had taken out of a chicken breast she had been give the day before (mistakenly).

When I arrived I was briefed quickly on the situation. I approached her inspection flap slowly and nervously, not knowing what to expect. When I looked through the flap Miss A was sitting on the bed crying, but when she observed me at her inspection flap she immediately started smiling. Her reaction made me feel more comfortable.

I asked her what the problem was. She replied, 'Tell these bastards who work on the seg to give me my tobacco back. Otherwise I'm cutting this tit straight off!' She had gone from smiling to anger.

I got her tobacco back from the seg offices and immediately returned it to her. Then she passed me the chicken bone that she had threatened to cut off her breast with. I was so relieved. It stopped me and other officers having to enter her cell. I really think every one of us was pleased. It would have been like trying to take a rhino down.

Over the years that Miss A spent with HMP Newhall she suffered a lot of neglect and lived in inhumane conditions. Yes, she was a very aggressive and dangerous woman, but she didn't deserve the treatment she was receiving.

Looking back, I can now understand why she would demand my attention. Without me she would have received no attention from any member of staff. I've seen dogs in the roughest homes looked after better than Miss A.

The next incident ended in an unnecessary fatality. There was a young woman in custody who had been admitted to Pinderfields Hospital, Wakefield. Protocol calls for two officers to keep the woman in custody while in hospital care. Normally one officer will chain themselves to the inmate using what called a closet chain. This chain is around 3 metres long. When the chain is on both your wrist and the prisoner's, it's then locked off by the other officer, and he or she keeps the keys for security reasons. On this occasion, a male and a female officer were on duty. The inmate asked to use the toilet, so the two officers escorted her while being secured on the closet chain. Once you arrive at the toilet the prisoner is allowed to go into the cubicle alone, but the closet chain is still attached. The cubicle door is closed, but the chain stops full closure.

At this point the officers have no eyes on the inmate, so to keep contact and control of the situation they give the chain a gentle tug and ask the inmate, 'Are you okay?' Normally inmates shout yes, but for some reason on this occasion the officers never tugged the chain or asked about her welfare. These two officers obviously were very complacent and not attentive to the situation.

After a long period of time had passed, one of the officers finally shouted, 'Are you okay in there?' There was no answer, so he tugged on the chain. To his great surprise, there was zero resistance. This could only mean one thing – thanks to their complacency, the inmate had escaped.

They immediately opened the toilet door to find the closet chain on the floor but no inmate. At this point I can imagine their heads were in a right spin. On this occasion the two officers were extremely lucky, because the inmate, during her attempt to escape the confinement of the hospital and the two officers, stopped the security officer at Pinderfields Hospital, who was driving around in a white Ford Sierra. 'Are you a taxi?' she asked. He replied 'Yes, jump in'. She did, and he drove her straight back to the ward, where the two prison officers were searching frantically.

You can imagine the disappointment on the woman's face when after all her efforts to gain freedom she was delivered back into the hands of two extremely relieved and thankful officers. The security man, Les Simms, was a close friend of mine. He told me later he recognised the inmate because he had seen her on his ward visits.

Later the woman told the officers she had escaped because she wanted to see her kids in Featherstone, she was missing them so much. The officers reported the incident back to the governor and the governor requested that the inmate be returned to custody in HMP Newhall. Upon her return she was placed on the segregation unit. She was emotionally upset and very depressed.

When an inmate is in a very low emotional state, all precautions are taken for their safety.

On this occasion the two officers failed to follow procedures or protocols. She was left with the belongings she had had in hospital, which included her dressing gown with a belt on it. I personally would have removed this garment for obvious reasons. The next morning she was found hanging in her cell.

So not only was the service negligent in not removing her dressing gown and belt, but this negligence led to the sad death of this woman. These items should have been removed on her arrival on the segregation unit. They were also negligent not to watch her through the night, knowing how low her mood was.

On the occasions I myself worked nights, one thing that sticks prominently in my mind is the OSG who worked on the segregation unit every two weeks. He would do a round on the segregation unit to check all inmates were present and correct. Then he would make his bed up in the office, then set his alarm – not to check on vulnerable inmates but to do his electronic pegging. This was a way the prison service could check that you were checking on inmates. However, all this chap did was touch the electronic pads, to make it appear he had checked on them. The 'round' would take him around five minutes, and then he returned to his bed.

The officer who was in charge (Night S.O.) knew for a fact that this particular OSG would sleep. We would only visit the segregation unit if the OSG contacted control to say there was a problem. Were the family get informed that the service was negligent? No.

There were many cases of negligence during my time in the prison service, and on some occasions I myself was guilty of being part of it. For instance, on one occasion three of us had to do a cell removal, which involves three officers putting protective equipment on, one acting as the 'front man' and the other two as wing men. Once the removal is complete, each officer should write a report on what exactly took place during the operation. Each report should be completed by each officer, with no interaction between officers. Then the reports are submitted to the governor in charge of the wing where the cell removal took place.

On every occasion when I took part in a cell removal, all the officers sat together and made the reports fit together. This means whatever happened within the cell, such as punching an inmate or kneeling on them, never gets reported because each officer checks none of the others is whistle blowing. Even if you witnessed abuse you can't report it, because if you did you would be ostracised.

I didn't agree with what was taking place. But did I want to be ostracised or lose my job? The pain and pressure the staff would have placed on me would have been too much for anyone to suffer.

CHAPTER 8

The dark side of prison life

I had several allegations made against me while in the female estates. They were all completely unbelievable and were seen by senior officers for what they were – rubbish. However when people throw shit, bits tend to stick. Then some people start to think 'Hey, people keep saying these things, Kev really is becoming a sex pest'. Then the whispers start. You become paranoid and the whole situation starts to take over your mind and your life. Your home life starts to go wrong. So by now you and the wife are at loggerheads and forever fighting. Then it's time for work, and you hate going. In the morning briefing, you feel like everyone is against you. You even feel dirty, like you really have crossed the line by having relations with an inmate.

The crunch came when I was on nights. Now I was in security, and anyone who knows anything about prison work will understand that on nights there is only one officer who carries cell keys, the security officer. I did two nights, and on the third night the senior officer who was in charge of the prison for that week approached me and said, 'I haven't told you, but you're under investigation'.

As you can imagine I was shocked and horrified. I asked who had put the allegation in and she gave me the name. I said 'I've been walking past her cell for two nights with the only cell key in my pocket.'

She said 'That's why I've told you Kev. You're too nice a guy for these bastards to hang you out to dry.'

I said I had never gone near any wings that night. The next day I rang the Governor and said I would be going sick with stress due to her being irresponsible and leaving me vulnerable. She was very irritated by my action, to the point where she and the deputy governor, who coincidentally were having an intimate relationship, decided to victimise me big time. They sent people to watch me while I was sick. Senior officers were ringing me three or four times a week putting me under pressure.

The police turned up at my wife's pub - I had no idea they were coming. I had organised a race day and I was giving all the lads their tickets and income the CID. 'Mr Kevin Graham?' they asked me.

I said, 'Who are you?' Think on this, it's 10 o'clock on a Saturday morning and these two strangers have just walked in.

They responded by saying it had been alleged that I had sexually assaulted a woman, and gave the name and date. Everyone was listening, and I felt so small. They told me to go on with my race day and report to Wood Street Police Station on Sunday morning at 10 o'clock.

I said, 'Do I need a solicitor?' He said, 'If it was me I would'. At this point my arse started to fall out. I was straight on the phone to a solicitor, who thankfully said he would meet me at Wood Street. On the Sunday morning I went to Wood Street, very apprehensive of what was about to happen to me. Upon arrival the sneaky cops invited me and my solicitor in through a pair of self-locking doors. Once we walked through these doors they locked them behind us. Only then did I realise these cops were just a pair of bastards. They went straight into reading me the riot act.

After about one hour, these two comedians finally let me see my brief. His advice was just to answer honestly. 'They have got nothing on you,' he said. My reply was, 'How can they even think they have anything on me? I'm totally innocent.'

With that, the Two Ronnies called me back into the interview room. About an hour later they said, 'We're going to bail you pending investigations'.

I walked out of Wood Street feeling like a dirty pervert. My wife was waiting for me. She was crying and I was near to it. It was at that point I knew I couldn't put this wonderful woman through anything like this ever again. I knew that whatever the outcome, I was packing this fucking job in, the sooner the better. Some things in life are worth more than ambition. After all, I came from nothing and I wasn't afraid to go back there.

There's an old saying, 'Be nice to people going up the ladder, because you never know when you may meet them on the way back down'.

The police investigated me for six months. My head was in a spin and I was deeply depressed. Life seemed so hard. Paula was in total shock and felt so dirty, and her home was turned upside down.

I had asked the police to interview two inmates who had witnessed everything I had done the day I was accused of sexually assaulting the other inmate. One of them refused to be interviewed, but the other girl gave me a shining report.

I was called back to answer to bail in the police station, and the CID said I was not guilty of anything and the case against me was being dropped.

My heart was thumping in my chest. My wife was sobbing, and I began crying. It felt like God had been looking down on us. Had I been found guilty, I had decided to hang myself, because I could not bring any embarrassment to my wife or my daughters. However, the decision went my way.

The Governor at New Hall contacted me to have an interview with her, so one week later I went to meet her. She was a nasty bitch who was now pretending she was on my side. I knew she was watching me and trying to get other allegations on me. She and the deputy governor, Mr Barber, were in league together and in bed together – yes, he had been tickling her for years. Need I say more. They had tried to frame me for crimes I had never committed.

I took them both to task with the area manager. The outcome surprised me. The area manager decided that because I was just an officer, my allegation against these two bullies counted for nothing. I was so hurt and upset with this immature decision. I decided at this point that there was no point carrying on my career in these extremely dangerous waters.

Over the next two years, these two idiots victimised another governor, Mark Brook. The outcome of his inquiry was totally different from mine. I believe this had to do with his status within the service. Soon after they were both found guilty of Mark's demise, their own was to follow. The area manager moved Governor Snell to Cambridge to lecture about the prison system. He moved the deputy governor, Barber, to work under him at head office. He also told him that he was forbidden to enter any prison for the next five years.

These two individuals were just evil. They seemed to get their buzz out of power, until a higher power smashed their careers, and hopefully their lives, to pieces.

This incident totally devastated my life. I loved my career in the prison service, and my intention had been to climb the promotion ladder all the way to governor. This was a massive turnround within my lifestyle and upbringing. The service was so prejudiced against people like me who had climbed out of poverty.

Throughout my working life I had always tried to be a hard-working individual. Unfortunately some people and some employers don't give you a chance to develop your career. They enjoy seeing people fail. How sad are these people to stop the progress of a working-class lad, but they did, My job became intolerable, and the pressure they placed on me was too much.

One day I was in security getting ready to take a prisoner to a hospital appointment. This was a familiar procedure – handcuffs, risk assessment, all relevant paperwork, then contact your partner to meet you in the reception. At that point the prisoner would show up at reception and an SO would go through the paperwork and lastly check the cuffs on the prisoner, then sign them into your safe keeping.

On this day, while I was still in security, the phone rang. It was my wife notifying my department that my stepdad had been rushed to hospital. My governor said 'Kevin, leave the escort and go straight away to the hospital to see your stepdad is okay'.

With that I dropped my bag and ran down to the gate. Once I got out of the gate I proceeded to my car. I drove like I was Michael Schumacher. When I landed at the hospital I ran into A&E and asked where Jack Rafter was. Straight away a staff nurse took me to one side and said 'I'm afraid that sadly, your dad has died'. I broke down in tears. I loved this man as if he had been responsible for my birth. People always say blood is thicker than water, but on this occasion that saying didn't even touch the surface. He loved me as a father loves his son, and in return I loved him as a father.

As I stood crying with the nurse, the prisoner and two prison officers walked through the doors. This was the escort I had been getting ready to take out when I got the bad news about my stepdad. The officers asked me what was wrong and I told them. Unfortunately their prisoner heard the conversation, as she was handcuffed to the officers. Bless her, she threw her arms around me and said, 'I'm so sorry for you Mr Graham, you're such a lovely officer!' Then she started crying.

That reaction towards me told me there is still love and affection within prisoners. It's not all about hatred towards other human beings.

The officers moved on with the inmate, and all of them wished me all the best. I asked the nurse to summon the Catholic priest, and she said 'no problem', but after 30 minutes he still hadn't arrived. I was so cross. I said to the nurse, 'Before I leave my stepdad's body I want him to receive the last rites'. Just as I was speaking the priest walked around the corner. 'Hello' he said, 'sorry I'm a little late.' I told him in no uncertain terms that my dad had been a staunch Catholic for 84 years, attending church every Sunday. 'So you show him the same respect as he has shown the Catholic Church for so many years'.

He bowed his head and said sorry. He then went into the room and gave my stepdad the last rites he had earned and deserved. I shook hands with the priest and left my dad in the hands of the hospital staff.

When I joined the prison service in 2002, my main reason was to try and bring some kind of help and understanding to those who for one reason or another found themselves within the justice system. Some would spend a significant amount of their natural lives within the 'big house' as we would call it, others for just a few months. The life these people were about to embark on was one of uncertainty, bullying and a 360-degree change in lifestyle.

From the first day, many inmates would be very nervous and apprehensive. Other more well-seasoned inmates would see an opportunity to exploit these poor individuals. If an officer had any interest in the wellbeing of nervous and apprehensive inmates they would make it apparent to seasoned inmates that they were giving these people their attention and consideration. This kind of care shown by an officer usually deters the more seasoned inmates from pestering a new arrival.

Once a new inmate is received and processed by the reception team, they are held in a mass holding room until he or she is allocated a cell. Once this process as been finalised by the control room, inmates would be escorted to their allocated wings. That's when the new inmates become aware of their new surroundings.

My job is to show due diligence once I enter the wing where new arrivals are settling into their new home. It's a 9 foot x 6 foot cell with a bolted-down single bed, 1x pillow, 2x sheets, 1x blanket, toilet, sink, and let's not forget the mirror. But best of all, a colour 14" TV. However this can be taken away if the prisoner falls asleep and leaves it on, or as a punishment for bad behaviour. This TV business was always a powerful tool for wing officers, but again this power made some wing officers even bigger bullies. I've seen countless TVs turned off with fish keys outside the cell, or removed for trivial things. To some officers, it's all about power.

On many occasions I've challenged bullying behaviour. I never reported one officer but I made them aware that if they repeated their behaviour I would take the matter to the governor. Needless to say I never witnessed a repeat of the same behaviour.

I personally found the biggest problem within the penal system was the Mr Mackays, as I would call them. I'm referring to the character in 'Porridge', the BBC prison comedy series starring

Ronnie Barker, where Mr Mackay, the officer in charge of the wing, played by Fulton Mackay, was a complete tyrant, obnoxious and one to stay clear of. These types were found in every prison I visited or worked in.

Of course, prisons shouldn't be seen as holiday camps, but having said that, in my opinion taking away a human being's liberties and locking them up in a cell is enough punishment for most offenders. But the prison service and its management won't listen to people like me, who have purposely joined their ranks to try to change the mentality of the officers. In some cases I believe I was successful. But in most cases I wasn't given a chance to even get close to the emotions of some officers. These people were, in my estimation, bullies.

I've witnessed many incidents that the prison service has covered up – and done so knowingly. There were matters such as a prisoner being treated disgracefully , and officers refusing to help the prisoner in any way. Then there were occasions when I witnessed bullying at its height, officers belittling prisoner in front of the whole wing full of inmates.

Undoubted the worst incident I personally witnessed was the bullying of a woman on the segregation unit. She was mentally impaired and in my opinion shouldn't have been placed on that unit. I spoke to management regarding Miss L, but they were not interested in her welfare, or really anyone's welfare, come to think of it. Miss L was being bullied by the two inmates whose cells were either side of hers. Things got so bad, with loud shouting and obscenities, that we were told to place a foam mattress against Miss L's cell door to try and block them out. She was constantly asking staff to see the governor to try and escape the bullying she was receiving 24/7.

But staff on the whole would not respond to these requests. They looked on Miss L as an idiot who was being locked away from society, so in their opinion she wasn't worth spending any time on. Staff would very often lie to her, saying 'yes, we've contacted the governor and they may pop down later to see you'. In reality they never even contacted a line manager, let alone the governor.

However I was present on the segregation unit when the duty governor attended. I brought the problem to his attention. He asked me to open her cell door, so firstly I had to remove the foam mattress. Once I gained access, Miss L was visibly upset and she pleaded with the governor to move her to the hospital wing. This was a wing where people like her were housed.

She was in floods of tears. The governor said 'There's no room on that wing'. Miss L said 'Please please, governor, I must move from this unit. These two women are bullying me, I'm wanting to move today.' She even said, 'Can't you get me into a secure unit somewhere? I will even sleep on a futon'. The governor laughed at this statement, but I thought it sounded alarm bells.

With that he walked out of the cell and she rushed towards him in frustration. I stopped her and appealed to her to consider what her actions would mean for her sentence. She broke down crying, but the governor just walked away. He showed no empathy or sympathy towards Miss L. She used a few choice words to thank the governor and say goodbye.

Once I'd calmed her down, she thanked me for my help and my consideration towards her. On that note I locked her cell door and went to the office to speak to the governor. Unfortunately he had left the segregation unit, but later that day I spoke to him in another part of the prison. I asked why Miss L couldn't be moved onto the hospital wing, as there was a cell spare. I insisted she was receiving bullying like I'd never witnessed before.

He said, 'When I feel it's the right time to move her Mr Graham, I will.'

I then tried to explain again what was happening to Miss L, but he stopped me in my tracks. He reiterated, 'I said I will move her when I feel the time is right. Is there anything else?'

When a governor says that it means politely 'Piss off'. So I walked away.

Later that week I was asked to cover the late shift on the segregation unit. This is where all prisoners have had tea and in reality that's their day over with, but one or more officers need to be present in case the inmate is needing assistance. On this occasion the responsibility fell to me.

When on the segregation unit the officer who's on duty gives you the handover, this relates to inmates behaviour and any problems they have incurred during their shift. On this occasion it was as I expected, the officer went on to tell me he had had trouble all day with the two bullies either side of Miss L. He said they had never stopped shouting obscenities at her.

I replied, 'Why are these two getting away with this bad behaviour?' The officer went on to say that the governor wouldn't transfer them to another prison. He said the situation would calm down. I shook my head in disbelief that a well-versed and experienced governor could even contemplate this situation getting any better.

With all that said, the officer left the segregation unit, and I took over the running of the unit. I firstly did my checks on all the inmates, then made sure all paperwork was up to date. Then the daily paper gets opened up and I sit at the desk and start reading to relax.

I was reading for approximately 15 minutes when a cell buzzer went off. I looked on the board which indicated which inmate was requiring me, and sure enough it was Miss L. I went down to her cell and opened the inspection flap on the door. I looked around the cell, but I couldn't see anyone. So I shouted 'Miss L, where are you?' She replied, 'I'm on the floor near the door'. I said, 'What are you doing on the floor?' She said 'I've got my cig in my mouth and thought you would give me a light.

I said, 'You don't need to lie on the floor with it in your mouth, you could have rolled it under the door'. She apologised straight away. I said 'There's no need to apologise, roll it under the door.' As I said this, the two idiots either side of Miss L started shouting 'Pass the officer your little comfort blanket, cry baby, cry baby!' Miss L started crying and became very emotional.

I told the two inmates to stop shouting or I would place them both on report. They quickly stopped. I then went back to Miss L to calm her down, and after speaking to her for about 15 minutes she started smiling again.

After this reaction I decided to have a little fun with her, so I said, 'Right Miss L, straight to bed now, no more buzzer for Mr Graham.'

She smiled and said 'I'm going to bed now, night night Mr Graham.'

I said 'Night night, and watch out because I might bite.'

She started to giggle. I found this reaction very rewarding and felt I had brought an enjoyable end to a miserable day for her. She climbed into bed, and that was the last time I ever spoke to her. The next morning the night officer found her hanging in her cell.

When I heard this news from other staff, I was shocked and disgusted. I had pleaded with the governor to move her onto the hospital wing and he had insisted that he would only move her when he was ready. Now that arrogant decision put her death firmly at his feet.

I now wonder what would be made of his decision by the number one governor. Shortly after the death of Miss L a prison service enquiry started into the reasons behind her death. Or should I say the cover-up surrounding her death, because deaths or incidents that could have been avoided were very often covered up to the prison service's advantage by management. And this incident was certainly one of those.

The two bullies who originally drove Miss L to take her own life were never mentioned in the report, nor was the governor's decision not to remove her from the segregation unit and the bullying environment she was suffering in. When Miss L's mother, father and sister were invited to meet the number one governor to discuss the death of their daughter, they were never given the true story surrounding her death or told of how she had pleaded with the management to move her away from the two inmates who had driven her to take her own life or of how she had died in desperation because of the bullying. No, they were told she had made numerous suicide attempts which had been foiled by the wing officers. However on this occasion she had used the cover of night time to fool them. I suspect this made her family feel a little bit better and more content that everything within the power of the prison service had been done. How misled this family were. Had these lovely people been given the correct information surrounding their daughter's death, they would have been fuming. They were an upper middle class family, so I have no doubt these people would have taken this matter further, and rightly so. But once again the management walked away unscathed.

The truth never came out regarding Miss L and her death. No officer within the establishment dared to breathe a word of what had really happened. Anyone who had would have been seen as a whistle blower, and management would have ruined their career.

Later in my career I saw this at first hand, but for now I have more information regarding cover ups that the prison service are guilty of.

Moving on, I would work night shifts around every three months.

Obviously prisons are much quieter on nights and it's very rare for there to be incidents due to the fact that 95% are in single cells. Unless you can fall out with yourself, then it's sleep time.

However, a skeleton staff of officers have a care of duty towards the inmates. They should always be kept safe, and electronic pegging takes place on every wing throughout the prison. This is designed to make sure officers don't sleep. Instead they must wander around the various wings using their electronic gun to make a contact with the electronic pegging point and also check on the 2052s, as they were called back in the day. In other words, a suicide watch.

An inmate may sleep like a baby, but if you don't check everything is okay and for some reason you find they have hanged themselves. Then I'm afraid your neck is on the line. But when I was on a night shift every officer would sleep, even the SO or the night governor who said to me, 'I'm going to sleep, don't bother me unless there's a death'.

Then they would walk off down the corridor with two pillows under their arms. Needless to say I would run the prison in the absence of the night governor and most of the officers. No one ever showed any compassion towards the highly vulnerable inmates.

On one occasion I remember well, I had to wake the night governor up because a very young girl had gone into labour. He wasn't best pleased because I woke him half way through the night. After I had explained the situation about three times, he sat up and pulled his boots on. We walked over to the wing, where the staff were waiting frantically for us to turn up, because only the night governor can open the gates, and only I can open cell doors.

When we arrived at the wing, a young female officer was saying 'We really need to get a move on because the baby's on its way'. The night governor said, 'Don't rush me for this waste of skin'.

I found that remark disgusting, and so did the female officer.

She said point blank to the night governor, 'You are disgusting'. He turned to me and laughed. I didn't know what to do, so I just said 'Look, let's get this kid out of here.

At this point I opened her cell. My God she looked shocking. Her hair was wet through with sweat and her face looked like she had been in a volcano. I asked the SO if he would go open the outer gate to give access to the ambulance that was on its way.

His reply was unbelievable. 'No,' he said, 'she can walk to the main gate.'

I replied 'No sorry, she can't be expected to walk in her condition.' But he was adamant she had to walk.

She was in really bad pain and was bent over crying. I bit my lip and said, 'You give me the keys and I'll run and open the gates'. He agreed to that suggestion, because it meant he wouldn't have to walk another 100 metres. However by taking his keys off his chain and handing them to me he broke with HMP protocol and procedures, and he was the acting governor. This kind of work ethic is found commonly within the service but rarely challenged.

One female SO, when working nights, would openly walk down to the comfortable tearoom with her pillow tucked under her arm shouting across the control room to me, 'Kev, you're in charge of the prison now, only wake me if there's a death'. And she sincerely meant those words. So I would take over any decision-making during her beauty sleep.

There was another female officer who would bring her weekly ironing for her and her partner. She would stand in the control room with an HMP ironing board and iron, not forgetting a basket of ironing which she had carried through the gate area and up to the control room. No upper management ever said anything to her regarding her blatant lack of responsibility towards inmates and staff.

Incidents like this one happened on a daily basis. One occasion that sticks in my mind went as follows. I was starting night shifts, and on the Monday night I turned up at the gatehouse and asked the officer for my keys. As he was getting them he shouted over to me, 'The Audley officer wants you to contact him straight away, he's in the control room'.

The Audley officer is the person who is in command of the prison until the night SO takes over command.

I replied, 'What's wrong now?'

The officer replied, 'I don't have a clue. He just seemed in a hurry to contact you.'

So with that I went to the nearest phone and contacted the Audley officer. He asked me to go to E wing to collect a girl who had smashed a coffee jar, then systematically slashed her arm. When I arrived, the afternoon staff were still present. They took me up to her room and asked her to accompany me to the health care centre. She wrapped a prison towel around her injured arm and came out her room.

We spoke quite pleasantly while walking to the health care. While we were talking she removed the towel and said, 'I've made a mess sir'. I looked and said 'Yes I really do think you have.' The slash was approximately seven inches long and it was so deep that all the layers of fat underneath her skin were exposed. The width of the slash was approximately one inch. So that's seven inches long and one inch wide. Now that is one hell of a self-harming injury.

However she was very good and not disrespectful, as a lot would not be in this situation. She wrapped the towel around the slash on her arm and we carried on to the health care. Once we arrived I spoke to the night nurse and explained what had taken place. She asked the girl to uncover the wound.

The girl took off the towel. The nurse looked at the wound , then she looked in disgust at the girl and said, 'What a bloody stupid thing to do on my first night shift!'

The girl apologised to the nurse, but she cut her off midstream and said, 'Don't start talking shit to me girl, you've ruined my first night.'

The girl just looked at me, as if to say, 'I tried my best'.

I asked the nurse to attend to the girl and said that then I would get her back to the wing, so she wasn't spoiling her night. She looked daggers at me. She had assumed I was taking the girl's side in this matter. To be honest I was, because the nurse's attitude towards the girl was so disrespectful. She might be a criminal, but let's not forget she was still a human being.

The disrespect went on even further. The nurse turned to me and said, 'Can you stitch?'

I said 'I've never had to stitch, I'm not medically trained.'

She said, 'When I complete a stitch you cut it, is that okay?'

I wasn't happy about this, but I wanted the girl attending to, so I said 'Yes, I'm fine with that.' Really my stomach was turning.

Then she went on to say, 'Before we start could I have a private word with you Mr Graham?'

'Yes,' I replied.

She took me to a quiet corner in the room, so the girl couldn't hear our conversation.

She went on to say, 'That idiot of an inmate has pissed me off doing what she has done to herself. So this is what I intend to do. Because this bag of shit has made us start working early, she will pay the price.'

I looked at her and asked, 'What exactly do you mean?'

'I intend to stitch half of the wound with anaesthetic administered, then the other half I will stitch without. She is having some pain for messing us around.'

I said, 'No, you can't do that!'

She replied, 'Oh yes I can.'

She walked over to the girl, who was in a great deal of pain. 'I'll stitch your arm, but the problem I'm having is I've only got enough anaesthetic for half the wound,' she said.

The girl said, 'I don't understand, what do you mean?'

The nurse looked daggers at the girl and said, 'Half the wound will be stitched with no anaesthetic, because I've not got enough in my cupboard.

By this time the girl was sobbing, with tears rolling down her face.

I said 'Surely nurse there's something else we could do to help this girl?'

'There isn't a alternative,' she said. 'Hold out your arm.'

The girl held out her arm, and the nurse thrust the needle straight in. I had taken hold of the girl's arm first. Thank God I did, because the way she administered it would have ended up being another disaster.

Once the anaesthetic was put into the girl's arm, the nurse started to get the stitching equipment ready. I was furious, this action, was so inhumane, and by a nurse of all people. I held the girl's hand and said, 'Look, just squeeze my hand if the pain gets too much'. She just looked and nodded.

The tyrant of a so-called nurse came over the chair were the girl sat terrified. She then began stitching. Each stitch was tied off and at that point I had to cut the stitch. The girl wasn't really feeling any pain – until it came to the last third of the wound. Oh my god she screamed. She squeezed my hand so hard I don't know who was feeling the most pain, her having no anaesthetic or me with my hand being crushed in her grip.

When this horrific episode was over I just said to the nurse, 'I hope you sleep well tonight'.

She knew what I was hinting at. I was thinking about any allegations that might be made by the girl. And all because the nurse's night had been disturbed.

I took the girl back to her wing and locked in her room, but before I left her I said, 'I hope I brought some kind of support to you tonight'.

'If it hadn't been for you and how you helped me I would have stabbed that nurse,' she said. And in hindsight, I truly believe she would have attacked that so-called nurse. Maybe by my patience I saved that nurse's life without her even knowing.

CHAPTER 9

Stitched up

———❧———

Unfortunately, after keeping my mouth shut and covering other officers' backs for years, my attempts to do a good job as a prison officer came back to bite me in the arse. Eight years down the line in my career I too became a victim of this uncaring, unprofessional, unethical service.

I was bullied and harassed by upper management.

I was suspended on a sexual allegation.

And I was investigated by West Yorkshire police, for six months, and by HMP.

At the end of all these investigations there was nothing to answer to, because I was innocent of all charges brought against me. I even had two inmates give statements to prove my innocence. At the end of my nightmare, the investigating officer made this remark: 'if one of those inmates that submitted evidence in your favour wasn't black, I would swear she was yours'. In my opinion this comment was racially driven and totally inappropriate.

I truly believe this so called police officer should have said that the two inmates who has given their support to me throughout this unpleasant situation should be given extra support for their honesty while their time is spent within the prison system, instead of making light of their honourable actions.

I was exonerated from all allegations made, but this didn't satisfy the two governors. They thought I was committing illegal activities, but in reality it was they who were committing illegal acts and breaking protocol and marital vows. However, the area manager and his cronies knew what was happening between these two governors. But no one wanted to be the whistle blower, so as usual they turned a blind eye to the situation. This attitude was rife throughout the prison service. From officers to upper management, no one dare break ranks. If you did you were instantly ostracised by the workforce and management would dish out more shit to force you out of the gate.

You will see from this book that I have had enough of this silence and of covering for people who can't even speak or smile when they see me in the street. This book is my platform to let the general public know how much deception and neglect goes on in those so called democratically run prisons.

I knew too much about their undercover affair. I had no intention of blowing their marital world apart, or their careers within HMP, but these two bullies thought differently. Their intention was to remove me from my job and my career, the thing that kept a roof over me and my wife's head. Not only were these two tyrants guilty of bullying and harassment, they were guilty of taking away a man's livelihood.

I took my case to tribunal on two occasions, but no incident could be identified by either judge. The first judge didn't read half the evidence I submitted. It was only when I asked for his reasons that I could see he hadn't read the evidence properly. I appealed his decision and suggested that its decision should be overturned on the grounds that it had been made on only half the evidence.

The tribunal said that even though the judge was guilty of lack of diligence, I still had to attend a second tribunal. I felt more comfortable at the second one and better listened to by the judge and the medical officer, but the outcome was just the same: no incident identified.

In my opinion the recurring incidents I was outlining to the tribunal were so obvious I really don't know how I could have described or explained them more clearly. I am of the strong belief that tribunals do not sit on the fence between employers and employees. I believe they are the government's way of giving the working man or woman a belief that we live in a democracy where we are protected by this farce called a tribunal service.

If a high-flying minister were to find himself or herself in the position I was placed in, barristers would be employed with solicitors assisting, and the bill for their work would come back to the taxpayer – the working man or woman, who gets no assistance with a matter that threatens their career. You just get kicked into the long grass, and if you're lucky you may be considered for universal credits.

Meanwhile the high-flying Cabinet Minister is sitting in his Chelsea gentleman's club drinking expensive brandy and smoking a Cuban cigar, surrounded by his cronies. These people live a privileged lifestyle. All these so-called ministers have to worry about is where the next million pounds is coming from.

What once could have been described as a democratic system is now revealed as a bunch of baboons sitting in privileged positions with too much money and too much power. In the words of the Native American: Only when every river is poisoned and all the trees are gone and no grass remains, only then will the white man understand you can't eat dollar bills. Or in our case, pound coins.

Before I left the service, I transferred to HMP Wakefield. I really thought Wakefield was a fantastically well-run prison – after all, it has seven hundred of the most dangerous men in Britain housed in there. It's the biggest category A prison in Europe. So I thought, this is the establishment for me.

The SO on the wing, Andy Murray, asked me, 'Would you like to explain why you're working here Kev, or do you want to see how things pan out?'

I replied 'No Andy, I would like to explain to your guys what I've been put through. I was totally innocent of what was alleged'.

Andy said, 'So when do you want to lay your case?'

I said, 'before unlock, after lunch'. He said that was fine. So when we came back to the wing after lunch, Andy gave the briefing, then went on to say 'Kev would like to explain why he is working here and not Newhall'. With that he handed over to me.

I stood up. I was immensely nervous, but I knew I had to address the officers. I went on to explain that a female inmate had set me up and made false allegations. I had had six months of hell while under investigation by the police and the prison service, and I had contemplated suicide if the police had pressed charges.

At the end of my speech, every officer had a blank expression on his face. Then one of them just shouted, 'right, shall we unlock?'

They left me standing there like I was guilty and should not be present on their wing. I looked at Andy. Had I said something wrong? He just looked at me and said 'sorry Kev'.

I felt so unwanted. At that point I wanted to walk out of the job I had dreamt of as a young man. Words can't explain how alone I felt. I had done nothing wrong but I was being persecuted by the officers and management I had left behind.

I went onto the wing to work, even though I felt sick. Those bullies had no idea how much pain I had suffered over the last six months while I was suspended . I couldn't live at home with my wife and teenage daughter because of the charges being laid against me. I had to leave all my friends at Newhall, which was hard because my mental state of mind was in pieces. Yet these officers carried on the harsh treatment I'd received from the two governors at Newhall.

I wandered around the wing in a daze. Then I started to notice even here at this massive Cat A prison there was bad practice. I saw an officer walking round the wing with a prison officer's hat on. Now these hats had been outlawed about 15 years before, because they were seen as intimidating to prisoners. This officer was wearing his hat on the wing, day in and day out, and nothing was ever said to him. Any inmate with an ounce of brains should have put a claim into the service for intimidation. And they would have won copious amounts of money. Then another officer was walking around the wing with a pair of Dr Marten's boots in highly polished red, not black as protocol demands. This was another establishment full of clowns, and I don't mean the prisoners.

After two weeks I could not stand the treatment I was receiving any longer. I reported to work and made my way to C Wing. The officers were standing in a circle, basically saying I was not welcome to chat with them. So I stood alone feeling like a piece of shit, but preparing to unlock.

When I arrived home, my wife asked why I was so upset. I told her the story about my afternoon with staff from hell.

She said, 'Don't go to work tomorrow'.

I said 'No, I've done nothing wrong, so why should I stay away? It's my career.'

She was in tears at this point because not only had I been through this injustice, she had too.

I reported for work the next day and once again I was ostracised by staff on C Wing. They stood in a circle talking on the wing before we unlocked, and I was standing alone just looking around.

Andy came out of his office and saw the stand-off between the officers and me. He turned to the circle of officers and said 'Come on guys, I know Kev is new on the wing, But please talk to him'.

With that comment one of the officers said, or should I say shouted, over to me 'We don't give a fuck about old officers'.

This comment just sent me off my head. I rushed over to the officer and stood right in front of his face and said 'I don't give a fuck about young officers!'

At this point Andy got between us both before we could both bring ourselves down to the level of the people we were locking up.

At this point I could not take any more pressure. I told Andy I had got to get off the wing and out of the prison. He tried to change my mind, but I was in a very dark and dangerous place in my mind. I walked off the wing and never returned to my job at HMP Wakefield. I had no intention at this point of leaving the service – I just couldn't stand the attitude and ignorance being shown to me. I decided to ring my line manager at Newhall to secure my return, because I relied on the job to pay my mortgage, car HP and basically to try and put my broken life back together. I thought she would be really sympathetic towards me, but how wrong I was. When I explained the conditions I had been working under at HMP Wakefield, she replied, 'You want to stop throwing your dolly out of your cot'.

I couldn't believe her attitude. Again she was another part of the management I personally covered up for, on nights when she slept while I took command of the prison, or through the day when she worked alongside me in security. Many times she would ask me to forewarn her if anyone was going to attend the fire officer's office, because he was her partner and many times she was feeling fruity and popped up to see him to have a little fun.

But this was the disgusting and disgraceful attitude I subjected to once again. And her attitude was driven by the two governors I spoke about. She did not dare cross them, otherwise her career would be smashed. So she tried her best not to let me back to the job where inmates and officers alike loved me. Yes, I had had a nasty allegation placed against my character, but that had been proven to be false and malicious. But management wouldn't let it go – they wanted my scalp. The pressure I was under from governors and senior management was pushing me to the edge. I couldn't take any more. I had to leave and try and sort my head out. 15 years on I am still suffering PTSD and having monthly conversations with my psychologist. Those monsters ruined my life and my blossoming career.

I hope this account of my own personal experiences has given you a clear picture of the reality of the atrocities and injustices that happen on a daily basis within the silent and secret walls of our penal system. To this day I can't believe I lost my career through such terrible behaviour by management and staff. All I ever wanted to do was make my colleagues happy and do my job well. I always took great care of the inmates and showed them compassion and empathy. So why did I ever deserve the treatment I received from staff and management?

My goal was to ride through the ranks to Governor grade. By achieving that position I would have fulfilled all my dreams within the service. Without blowing my own trumpet, I believe I would have run a prison to the standards that I feel are being missed under current management.

Our prisons must be run on mutual respect between inmates and staff, not by bullying or demoralising inmates. The staff under me would be better trained in inmate awareness and respect.

I'm not saying for one minute that we should start running prisons like Butlins without beer, but too many officers, young and older, put their uniforms on before coming to work and immediately turn into Nazi Blackshirts. Many times I've told young officers they should never speak to inmates with attitude, but they only took notice while I was around. As soon as my back was turned they would carry on as before. An establishment that could stop this kind of approach to inmates would be very successful, and the more successful you are the less money it costs the country. But I will never be in a position to run a prison, thanks once again thanks to the bullies in management.

Now eleven years have passed and unbelievable pressure has been placed on me. I have suffered mental illness, nightmares and lack of self-respect, all thanks to the prison service and its henchmen, or 'governors' as they call them. I believe they drummed me out of the service with no duty of care or any thought for my welfare.

I appealed against their decision and on April 26 2018 I attended a tribunal at Leeds magistrates' court. The judge at the tribunal decided that there was nothing for the prison service to answer to. I took his comments on the chin and awaited his reasons in writing. When I read these reasons it was obvious to me that he had not read all my evidence, so I appealed his decision and approximately a month later the courts agreed with me, saying there had been an error in law.

The tribunal was fair and the judge and doctor gave me plenty of time to present my case, approximately one and a half hours. I really thought I had won the case, but no. The Judge contacted me two days after the hearing to say he couldn't find an incident.

Now leaving an officer with cell keys on night duty with a sexual allegation hanging over his head to me spells out a negligent attitude by the Governor. Or in technical terms, a lack of duty of care. But the

Judge couldn't see that. Allegedly.

I truly believe the law in this country is fine for people who can afford fat cat barristers. It is not designed for the working man.

But somehow, had to move on. My wife and I decided to go back into the licensed trade.

CHAPTER 10

Life after prison

—◇—

We took a pub, and battled to make it work for three years. We met a lot of wonderful people and a lot of nasty people. One lad who will always remain in my heart and my thoughts was Steve Railton. He became very sweet on Hannah, and I think Hannah was sweet on him, but she was excellent at disguising it. However, after two or three weeks she weakened and fell for him. He was a lovely lad. He helped me in the cellar at the pub, and he would do anything for me. He was a very good worker. Every day he went off making concrete posts and delivering them to customers. Then he would come home from work, get a shower and changed, then come straight down to the pub to meet Hannah and help me and Paula.

Once Paula and Hannah went away to Spain for the week, and Steve moved into the pub with me. Every night he helped me. Then he would fly off in his car and on his return he would have a bag in his hand and say shall I put this Chinese out, Kev?

At that point he would have the biggest smile on his face, knowing I would be pleased with our supper. We would kick all the punters out and get the plates out, then sit and laugh and enjoy every mouthful.

When Hannah and Paula returned from Spain, we all decided

Steve should move in with us. We all got on like a house on fire, until Steve and Hannah fell out and didn't speak for quite a while. They made up again, but then they fell out again. It was like watching a bloody tennis match.

Then suddenly, while they were both secretly talking, Steve decided to take his brother Sam to college in his car. Unfortunately the car hit a kerb and turned over. Sam got out of the car unmarked, but Steve wasn't that lucky. The roof of the car had creased when it rolled and punctured Steve's head, killing him outright.

Sharn rang to let us know what had happened. Hannah went to pieces, screaming and shouting. It took a long time to console her and calm her down. We were all devastated, as Steve was like a son to me and Paula, and I have no doubt a future husband for Hannah.

Steve lived with his mam, Julie, and unfortunately we had fallen out with her. I said to Hannah, 'we need to see Julie'. We went and bought her flowers and turned up at her house. Sam was crying. I knocked on the door and said how sorry I was about Steve. I hugged Sam, and Julie was sobbing. I went on to say 'I will fully understand if you tell me to bugger off', but she threw her arms around me and kissed me, and I kissed her back. I apologised for falling out with her and her family and invited them to the pub for drinks. She accepted my offer, but never came down. She and all her family fell out with me and my family, and unfortunately we have never spoken again. But that will never change my love for Steve. He was the son I never had. God rest you son.

There was a bizarre episode roughly one month after Steve's death, in our bedroom in the living quarters of the Royal Oak, Crofton. Our little Jack Russell Terrier, Tiny, was going crazy at the wardrobe in our bedroom. I went in to see what the problem was. At first I thought a rat had sneaked into our bedroom. I removed the dog to investigate the problem. I pulled the wardrobe out and to my surprise a young starling was behind the wardrobe, so I helped the little bird to get out. I opened the bedroom window and stood back to let it escape. As the little bird flew out from the wardrobe it perched on the curtain rail and looked me in the eye for at least a minute. Then it suddenly flew out of the window.

I dashed to the window to see where the bird had vanished to. It flew into the distance until I could no longer see it.

Now the bedroom widow or any windows had not been opened for months, So how did that little bird get access to our living quarters? That was a mystery.

I feel that little bird was Steve reincarnated, and he wanted to say goodbye. I cried like a child, feeling it was Steve. I know that lad would have gone out of his way to say goodbye, and to this day I believe it was him.

Shortly after this wonderful experience of seeing my lad fly off to rest, I was presented with another massive blow: I was diagnosed with Parkinson's disease. That finished our career and our life and brought our efforts to an abrupt end. Since then I have had a massive back operation that has left me with screws in my back to secure it. I walk around on a morning like Robocop. I still have a great deal of pain, and it seems to be worse at night.

Three weeks after my op I suffered a stroke. This has again changed my life for the worse. If I get a headache I worry that it's the start of another stroke. I have lost short-term memory and it is difficult to remember people's names.

Life was great once upon a time, but now it feels like I've killed a nest full of robins. However because you walk, talk and breathe normally, people think there's nothing wrong with you and tend to talk about you like you're some kind of scrounger off the state.

People never look at all the work and money you have put into the country. Instead they assume you want to live the easy life. May I say I would have worked until I dropped until I had completed my working career, but Parkinson's took this away from me. I sat for endless days at home feeling sorry for myself after this onslaught of medical conditions hit me. It felt like I would never work again. However, Hannah was working for Access Hire as a receptionist. This was a very busy cherry picker van business which delivered vans throughout the UK to businesses city councils and BT yards, to mention a few.

Hannah could see how disappointed I was to end my working life so abruptly, so she made enquiries at work as to whether I could do a little part-time driving for the company.

Shortly after she enquired, I was invited to speak to the transport manager, Les Cunningham – what a great fellow. He listened to me explaining my situation and said, 'Kevin, don't worry about any medical problems. Do you feel you could drive and deliver these vans?'

I said 'obviously Les, I'd love to be given an opportunity'.

'Then come in tomorrow at 7 am and let's get started'.

I felt like Les had just pulled me out of a sludge-filled pond that was gradually pulling me under.

All the guys who drive the vans at Access Hire made me feel really welcome, even the owner, John Woods. He was – and is – a great boss who always has a laugh and a joke with me when he sees me at work. I believe his attitude is the reason he's been so successful in business.

There are quite a few characters who help to make the working day pleasant. Daz Roberts – I've had some great days out with Daz, laughing and joking all day long. Policeman Pete is a guy with a sense of humour that's drier than a bucket of sand. Ray Crossley, the man born with a shuffle walk who's in a rush to get home to his cat. That's the only pussy in his life...

Gadge, or Gary, the hoist inspector, loves to get his head in the clouds on one of his bucket inspections. This height away from all the moaners gives Gary sanity. He knows every cloud has a silver lining.

Ray Evans, or Sos – I'm sure Lester Piggott would have a bigger vocabulary than Sos. He made me think I needed a hearing test. While travelling around the UK with Ray he very rarely speaks, so I imagined I had lost my hearing, but no, it was just Ray, lost in his little fishing world.

Tony Dunhill, the man with a plan. Tony, forget the plan, stick to driving the van. He is the only person I know who argues with his sat-nav. Top man.

Steve Bolton. This guy is a reincarnated Formula One driver. Steve could strike a match on the boot of the car in front of him. Benny Hill once sang a song that reminds me of Steve – 'Ernie, the Fastest Milkman in the West'.

Some more of my great workmates:

Mark, new guy onboard, sound as a pound.

Mr McDonald, Alan Brown. This fella sniffs around until he finds work. He'll drive and skive behind a fatburger at any remote sarnie shop. But he's punctual, that's a good thing, Al.

Brian and Chris, the mechanics. Both excellent blokes, maybe not the best looking but who gives a shit when every van starts first time.

All the valeting gang, Danny, Chris and Jim, good lads, good team if they were playing darts, because they are shit with the polish and cloths. Or at least that's what Les said.

Last of all Les, the most controversial transport manager you will ever meet. If he says good morning I go straight outside and see if it's light. He would fall out with himself in an empty room. But if you catch him on a good day, He may smile while he's making you look silly in front of your workmates. Les is the best boss I've ever worked with. He doesn't suffer fools or arrogance within his workforce, and he doesn't stick to PC rules. He says it as it is.

He has one rule for the orders he barks out to the workforce: like it or leave it. I think bosses don't come any more direct than that. Nevertheless I admire Les and his way of working. If this country was blessed with more people like Les, it would a better place to work and live in.

So I would like to take this opportunity to thank everyone at Access Hire for giving me a chance to continue to work and to enjoy my working life.

My greatest friends in life are very few, So I will name them:

James and Alison Swannell with their baby girl Rachel – more about them shortly.

Johnny Scuffam, mentioned earlier, has been a friend since we were nine years old. Without him and Steve Tottey, my life would have been like living in a monastery. I never had any problems with Johnny – we grew up like brothers. In fact I think we're closer than most brothers. We both had hard childhoods. We worked on the milk deliveries around Crofton for approximately two years, getting out of our lovely warm beds at 5.30 am in the pouring rain to deliver milk. It takes a lot of willpower. Did I mention Johnny is short on willpower? So many times I had to go to his house and throw stones at his window. Eventually he would shout 'Yer yer, I'm coming'. Then a cig and a coffee later we would head off to Peter Bain's farm, where Peter was sat waiting for us.

The next two hours were hard, to say the least. Eventually we'd return to the farm and by then we had woken up. It was now around 7.30, so we both walked home to get breakfast, then off to school. Very often we would call at my house, eat cereals and crash out in a chair. School was put on the back burner many times. We had our share of stick off the headmaster for truancy and turning up late, but hey ho, we got our £3.50 a week.

Johnny took a job at a potato farm and later that year he got me a job there too. It lasted one day. They needed the world's strongest man, not me. I had to open 56lb sacks of potatoes and throw them on my back, then empty them into a large hopper. The first 50 bags weren't bad but after that I was carrying them 40/50 yards to the hopper. By the end of the day I was knackered.

I told Johnny after work, 'Tell your boss tomorrow I won't be coming again'. He just laughed. Then to add insult to injury, Johnny's boss never paid me for the one and only day I worked.

Johnny was the first of us to suffer illness. At the age of 27 he suffered an embolism on his brain. This was hard for him to take, because he had always been a fit young lad and a fit young man. But no one knows when tragedy and illness is going to hit us. We have to deal with whatever nature throws at us. Johnny fought against adversity and came out the other side of life a better man.

Johnny has always been my close and loved friend. Throughout life we've both had our ups and downs but he has help me through my back issues and psychological problems, and will always remain close to my heart. I will never meet a friend as honest and caring, in this life or the next. Thank you, Johnny.

Steve too had adversity to face in later life. After serving nine years in the Marines, he came home to settle down with His girlfriend, Julie Sidebottom. But what was to come for Steve no one could have predicted. He suffered a massive stroke, and to this day he lacks mobility in his arm and leg. Steve was probably the fittest lad in Crofton – you don't manage nine years in the Marines unless you're super fit.

Both of these two mates had extremely lovely mothers. I feel I should give these two outstanding women a mention. Johnny's mother Mabel, was a very educated women who could baffle us young lads with words. She demanded respect, and by god she got it. She brought up four children single-handed and with very little money. We all loved her in our own way.

Steve's mother, Bessie, was one lady no one crossed. She was very loving and helpful. Her love for Steve was constant. She also gave me love and happiness at a low time in my life. Thank you Bessie.

Talking about friends, the Swannell family I referred to above were great friends, and still are. So here's an insight into this lovely family. We were friends from a very early age. Ali and Paula are like sisters. They grew up together and have shared many holidays together. Alison's mum and dad, Ken and Madeline, were a lovely couple, and they treated Paula as another daughter. Alison and Paula enjoyed each other's company so much they would spend school holidays together. Memories are made of times like these, and I know these two share some wonderful memories.

Obviously I did know Alison as a child but later in life I was to meet her and her intended husband, James. They had great times together, and when Ali married James he and I became instant friends. He was always laughing and joking about something, so one day I decided to have a joke on him. I took him grave-digging one day, and his hair looked like the bloke in the film 'Beetlejuice'. When he plucked up the courage to start digging the grave I waited while his back was turned, then tickled his neck. He nearly jumped straight out of the grave. When he saw it was me he called me all the names under the sun.

Paula and I lost contact with the Swannells for about 12 years. Then out of the blue an old lady in Walton said she had been contacted by someone in Australia looking for me and Paula.

I asked, 'did they give their name?' The lady went around the houses before she finally got to the name I was desperately waiting for. Then that magic name came out of Miss Maples' mouth: Swannell, James and Alison.

I think I nearly fainted. I said, 'do you have their number?'

'Yes.'

'Then please give it to me.'

She gave me the number. After thanking her I turned to Paula and told her the news. She said 'pass the phone', then she rang the number and she was talking to our lifelong friends James and Alison. This was a massive breakthrough.

Soon after the call, James sent me and Paula two E-Tickets to fly out to Australia. Thats how close we always were. We had a wonderful month with three people we have always loved. Our relationship has deepened and we have visited time and time again. We've all decided that we are family. I can't thank James and Alison enough for the hospitality they showed me and Paula. They paid for days out and gave us a company car to use for the entire holiday period. No one could ever complain how they looked after us.

However, after this things for me took a big dip. My health started to suffer huge problems. I now suffer from Parkinson's disease, I've had a stroke, and I've had to have a massive operation on my lower back, where a titanium structure has been inserted in my spine.

I also have heart problems, by which I mean heartache. The biggest I have ever had has been the loss of my parents.

My father left us in 1988. That was one of the most hurtful times in my life. I loved him as I had never loved anyone. He inspired me to be honest, and most of all to be me. He was a father to look up to, without any doubt in my heart. God bless Dad.

The next major disaster in my life was the death of my mother, my guiding angel through life. Her love for me was second to none. The nine months I grew inside her were my time in heaven. Then I was born into hell.

My mother gave birth to me on the 4th of May 1959. She left me alone in this world in 2006 after suffering a massive stroke which wiped out the left side of her brain. She was taken from her home to Pinderfields Hospital, where she lasted for only five days. She was totally out of it. There was no way you could communicate with her, nor could she communicate with you. However to this day I think she understood what was happening around her, because we openly discussed her condition with a doctor. I told the doctor that my wife and me and my sister would meet him tomorrow before visiting time to discuss my mother's stroke. I genuinely believe she heard the discussion and at that point she knew death was imminent.

We kissed her and left for home. The next day we returned for our meeting with the doctor. Paula and her sister started to take their coats off and were talking away, but I looked at my mother and she appeared to be struggling to breathe. So I grabbed her hand and she squeezed mine. I bent over her and whispered in her ear, 'Mam, it's time to go, don't fight it'.

She took a sharp intake of breath... and then stopped.

I looked across at my sister. I didn't want her to know her mother had just passed over, because I knew her reaction would be to shout or scream and I didn't want her to shock my mother back. Paula was aware of what had just happened, but she kept quiet for me.

After a couple of minutes I broke the news to my sister, and as expected she started screaming and grabbed my mother around her shoulders.

I believe my mother waited for me to kiss her and wish her on her way. God bless you and keep you, mam. One day I will join you both in the after life. I will always be your son.

So my work and family life were hard, very hard. The whole thing was like being given three life sentences in hell, instead of three siblings. My sister Christine, in my opinion, loved me and only followed their lead because it was easier on her. So I forgive you, Christine.

Forgiveness for my brothers, Trevor and Melvin, for their conduct towards me as a child is something I have found more difficult. Unfortunately Trevor died on April 8 2020, and that was the most distressing time I've experienced. I hadn't seen him or visited him for about ten years, but having said that, we didn't have cross words. We just didn't live in each other's pockets. He always said 'If you need me I'm always there for you' and I said basically the same.

One day out of the blue, my sister Christine rang me to say she had seen Trevor in the doctor's and he didn't look very well. He was complaining he had no appetite and consequently he had lost a vast amount of weight. So later that night I rang him and arrange to visit him.

What a change in my brother. He had gone from a handsome, tanned chap to a frail and pale old man. I sat and chatted to him about his illness, and he knew exactly what was going on. He had read the report from the consultant. It wasn't good; he was riddled with cancer. They had found it in his liver, chest and various other places within his body. So as you can imagine, his mood was very low. I tried to make him laugh and generally cheer him up. Maybe I was a little successful, but under the circumstances I could understand his frustration.

We spoke about childhood stories, and that raised a smile. I suddenly felt overwhelming emotion coming over me, so I grabbed his hand, looked him in the eye and said, 'If I could do anything to turn back time for you, I would. I would have a limb removed if it would stop your pain problems.

He looked at me in a very loving way and said, 'I know you would'. I looked again into his eyes and said 'I love you', and he repeated 'I love you'. As brothers we had never spoken like this to one another before. This statement was so uplifting and positive. I felt we had finally become one.

I left on that note. As I was walking out of the house Jean, Trevor's wife, tried to ask me about his well-being. I couldn't even talk – I was in floods of tears and sobbing like a child. I found it so difficult to drive home.

Paula was waiting for me when I walked through the door, and she couldn't believe the impact Trevor's illness had had on me. She kissed and cuddled me. Believe me, I needed all her love and affection and she gave me every drop she had, bless her.

After this occasion I visited Trevor nearly every day. He had gone further downhill every time I saw him, until one day Jean rang to say, 'You need to come up to our house now, Kevin. He's slipping away'.

I immediately jumped into my car and sped up to Trevor's house. On arrival you could feel the mood in the house was low. I made my way to Trevor, who was in a bed downstairs. He was struggling to breathe and looked like something out of a horror movie. His eyes were bulging, and his face was like a skull. This was a man who was fighting for his life and losing.

Trevor's son Shane and I sat with him throughout his ordeal.

This was the first and probably the last time Shane and I cried in front of one another, even though Shane and his dad hadn't seen eye to eye, in front of him his father was struggling to hold on to his life. In my opinion that's enough to wipe any slate clean, however dirty it is. And that's what Shane did. I'm so proud of Shane for his behaviour on that heartbreaking day. It took a special kind of man, and that's Shane.

After approximately two hours of sitting with Trevor and talking about the past and present to our Shane I was once again overcome with emotion. I stood up, grabbed Trevor's hand and looked him straight in the eye. I said, 'I can't watch you like this anymore Trev, please go on your journey'. My tears were dropping on him. I let go of his hand and made my way to the door. Once again I couldn't speak to the family – I was in pieces.

As I walked through my door at home, the phone was ringing. Paula answered it. I could tell by her reaction that Trevor had died. When she came off the phone she said, 'Jean says he must have died as you left the room'.

I hope from the bottom of my heart that Trevor heard me asking for him to give up his fight and drift off back to our mother and father in the afterlife that waits for us all. Hopefully he will have taken my love with him on his journey through eternity.

Because of the Covid crisis we were enduring at the time of Trevor's death, we had to wait nearly a month for his cremation at Pontefract Crematorium. That day was unbelievable. Jean's family were all close and loving towards their mother. On the other hand, Christine and Melvin sat at the opposite side to me in the crematorium. They never spoke to me or embraced me, even when I stood alone with Trevor to give him my final farewell, neither of them flinched. They sat throughout the service like two blocks of stone. So once I'd said my farewell to Trevor I decided to leave the service without speaking to anyone. I made my way to my car and drove away in tears, with a broken heart.

When I got home Paula was waiting for me with bated breath. She immediately embraced me and once again she helped me to cope with the overwhelming stress and emotion I was going through.

When I informed her how Christine and Melvin had behaved throughout the service, she was astonished that two siblings could show so little emotion towards their younger brother. Paula was disgusted by both of them.

This behaviour prompted me to write a letter to Christine and explain how hurt and upset I was with their behaviour towards me. I ended the letter by saying 'It's now time Christine for you and Melvin to detach from me and my side of the family'. I suggested she should look after her side of her family and I would look after my side.

I now look at life from a different angle. There's always a silver lining in every cloud, or at least that's what my mother always said to me. And believe me that is true, because she could always get the best out of the worst situation. Mother was a great believer in the old world philosophy, and she had all the answers in abundance.

When Trevor was fit and well, he would go to Blackpool with mates, let's say 'mature' people, from Crofton once a year. They would all get very excited about Blackpool, especially when it was creeping nearer to October. The trip would normally take place around Trev's birthday, October 11th. Because it would have been Trev's 70th birthday that year, I decided to attend the gathering. However my main intention was to take a small portion of Trevor's cremated remains with me and scatter them in the sea at Blackpool. This was because Trev had loved the sea, and loved Blackpool.

So on the very day Trevor would have been 70 years old, October

11 2020, I took his ashes and a gang of Trevor's pals with me to the central pier. As we all walked across the sands to engage with the sea, I looked at the seven of us and thought, this could be a re-run of the Magnificent Seven. We would have been the oldest Magnificent Seven ever seen, but who else would get out of a warm bed at 7.30 in Blackpool on a cold October morning to go down to a windy beach and witness a scattering of remains? There are very few who would honour a friend like they did.

Once we reached the water's edge, we had to place ourselves strategically due to the wind. Anyone standing downwind would be getting an unpleasant early breakfast. We all said our goodbyes to Trevor, and then I scattered his ashes. I was so emotional I felt embarrassed, but there was no need. Each and every one of Trevor's old mates rubbed me on the shoulders and placed their arms around me. So I would like to take this opportunity to thank each person for there compassion: Ian Endersby, Johnny Scuffam, Chris Saberton, Billy Bennion, Paul Simmons and Mick Moore.

A special thank you to Ian Endersby. Because Ian was staying in a separate hotel, he had to run for 15 minutes to attend the scattering. Ian was 62, and shall we say he doesn't suffer from bulimia. I think you get the picture. I found his actions highly commendable. Ian mate, you're a star.

We all walked back to our hotel and sat down to breakfast. I found it difficult to eat mine. I felt like I was eating Jaffas, my throat felt so tight and narrow.

Later we all met at the H & A social club for a Sunday afternoon drink. I bought a round of shorts and when they arrived at our respective tables I stood and said, 'A big thank you to all the lads for attending Trevor's scattering'. And we all said together, 'God bless Trev'. We lifted our glasses and in one gulp we threw the shots down.

I personally don't drink whisky, but on this occasion I did. That was a day to remember, and Trev was a brother never to forget.

The next day we were leaving, and I felt as if I was leaving my brother helpless in Blackpool while I returned to my life in Wakefield. It wasn't a nice feeling. But in the words of Freddie Mercury, the show must go on, and unfortunately it must. Our Trevor rests in Blackpool, but there will always be a piece of him in my heart. God bless Trev. It was difficult to move on and find a happy place in my life, but luckily for me I had my own immediate family.

The only thing that ever kept me smiling was my family – my three beautiful daughters, three fantastic grandsons and two granddaughters. It just shows how from one young man like myself a massive expansion of family emerges. It's like throwing a pebble into a pond. The ripples that emerge from that impact on the water are like the kids that emerge from you as a person.

There's always one grandchild that stands out. Yes, I have that problem, he's a wonderful and remarkable lad. His personality shines so bright, if it was sunshine it would blind any normal human being. He is intelligent and active, and he's someone I will always love and be proud of.

He was born into this world on the July 6 2013, and he weighed 6lb 7oz when he was wrapped in a towel by a midwife and handed to me. I was in shock because I thought the baby would go straight to its mother. On this occasion that wasn't so, as his mother was shattered after his birth, so Grandad took over on motherhood duties.

That lad captured my heart from the minute he entered this cruel and hard world. I asked my daughter his name, she shouted across the room, 'It's Max, Dad'.

I looked at him and said 'Max, I love you'. And I don't think I will ever lose this overwhelming feeling of love for my little Max. He will always be my shadow in life and I will always be in his debt for giving me a lifetime of pleasure. There will be times when I'm sure it will be down to me to keep the lad in shape with attitude and manners, but whatever takes place over your lifetime, Max, always remember I will always love you and cherish you. Always remember the three rules of Grandad's law in life. 1: always listen. 2: always use good manners. 3: help elderly people when they're struggling. Smiles, and manners will open doors in life that you will never imagine. So please live your life to these rules.

My daughter has now given us another child. She has named her Minnie after Paula's late grandmother. This little girl is the most pleasant baby I have ever seen or been around. She has beautiful eyes and lovely soft skin. She was born on October 29 2017, and if her future is as bright as her smile, then what a future she has in front of her. Two beautiful kids with hopefully beautiful futures to look forward to.

I often wondered when my future would brighten, but luckily for me I have had someone by my side for many years and hopefully for many more. She's feisty, loving, and the best friend I ever had in life.

Now here's my appraisal of my lovely wife. Paula Dwyer-Brown has throughout been my rock to cling to and my salvation for life. She will always be a diamond to me. Unfortunately some people close to her wouldn't let her shine like the diamond she was, even as a child. Her mother never let her shine, yet underneath is a beautiful stone that is priceless to me, if not to her. Lots of mothers and fathers never see, or look for, the potential a child possesses. I find that unbelievable, and so sad, because to inspire and love a child gives that little life the chance to grow and blossom into a caring, considerate person. This process doesn't take your life savings, only your love.

Fortunately Paula had a damn good grandma and grandad to

show her love and surround her with happy thoughts and pleasant memories. From the bottom of my heart, thank you Bernard and Minnie Dwyer. Without you I would never have been given this remarkable, loving, caring girl, who grew into such a beautiful wife and mother. Thank you for your love and support, and most of all thank you for coming into my life and rescuing me from the depths of despair all those years ago. I love you for you and for that beautiful heart you give to me every day, week and month through all the years we have had together. If this world had more Paulas it would be a utopia for the male population. I never won the lottery or the pools, but I did win Paula. That to me is a bigger win than any of the above could ever give me.

CHAPTER 11

Looking back

—◇—

I'm writing this on the first day of a new year, 2021. Hopefully it won't be as bad as 2020, the year when the Covid pandemic hit us. The death count in China, where it began, has been unbelievable. When it hit our shores panic broke out among families, workforces and society in general. Strict measures were put in place by the new Conservative Prime Minister, Boris Johnson, and the country was locked down, closing schools, shops, pubs, clubs, theatres, restaurants – everything. Only essential shops could stay open. This was a time of exceptional worry, stress and boredom. After the lockdown period ended things began to improve, but in some parts the situation had got ridiculously bad, due to people not taking Boris and his team seriously. So from that pandemic first hitting our shores in March we have now suffered 500,000 deaths, with hospitals at bursting point, and to put the icing on the cake a stronger strain of the COVID-19 appeared. There was a race to develop vaccines to combat this bloody virus, which had caused untold hardships to every single person in this country and the world at large. Since then Covid has become more manageable, though it still refuses to go away.

Thank you for reading my story, of a lifetime of so many mixed emotions. Before I sign off I would just like to leave you with my view and take on life.

Always remember to treat everyone with respect and love. My mother always said manners cost nothing.

Listen before you speak – you gain knowledge this way and knowledge is power, especially in the home and workplace. And these two places are where we all spend most of our lives.

Empathy and sympathy towards others is a gift which will always be admired in you by others.

And above all remember you have one shot at life – there's no such thing as a rehearsal.

I have always believed that your life is a map built just exclusively for you. However you try and deviate from this map, it drags you back to sail your original course. So when you think things aren't working out for you don't worry, because somewhere in that hidden life's map your path will cross into paradise just make sure you hold on to that piece of paradise.

Don't become curious and start looking further into your map, because this will lead you back to a place you or your family won't want to be.

So the moral of the story is, when you find in life what you're looking for, look no further. In 1976 Rod Stewart released a fantastic record that related to the death of a friend. The friend was called George, and he was stabbed to death in New York for being gay. I quote: 'Youth's a mask and it don't last, so live it long and live it fast'. That line is a great reflection on life. Rod has fantastic lyrical skills, and every song relates to his experience in life. And that man had more than his share of experiences. So follow your dreams and your heart, make this life a wonderful time for you and those around you. This life isn't a rehearsal.

I hope my grandchildren have a wonderful life and are showered in finance, happiness and love.

I have now passed 64 years old. My last birthday was the worst I had ever endured. I felt so down and miserable to think of all the effort I had put into work and life, yet I still appear to be struggling.

Maybe how I started out in life was a indication to how I was going to finish it. Even so, you feel like the world has a problem with your prosperity, never mind your family. Unfortunately that's a battle I will have to fight to the end.

I would like to leave a tribute to friends and family who I have known throughout my life. These people played a massive part in my life, whether they are friends or members of my extended family. The names below will always have a place in my heart. God rest them all.

One friend in the list below stands out. I feel I have to speak more about Peter Crossland before I wrap my book up and finally put my memories to rest, so here goes. I first met Peter when I was about thirteen years old, when he and his wife and their son Tony lived in a terraced house at the back of my father's newly bought terraced house on Slack Lane, Crofton. Peter had just completed a stretch in HMP Manchester, otherwise known as Strangeways. His crime was doing wage snatches and blowing safes. While he was doing time in Strangeways, two more inmates accused him of grassing them up to the officers. Consequently the two inmates got more time on their sentences. However when they were released they drove over from Manchester in a Jaguar and arrived at Peter's house at 2 am.

They knocked on his back door. Peter answered the door, which had the chain lock on so it only opened slightly, but as soon as the door opened one of the men let two barrels off at Peter from a shotgun. Peter was shot in the side of his body. The men ran back to the Jaguar and fled the scene.

The police and ambulance attended. Peter was taken to hospital and luckily he survived the vicious attack by those two clowns who had nearly robbed us of a great pal and a husband and dad. They were caught and spent a long time in HMP Manchester, while Peter recovered and returned home. He soon returned to his old humorous self. He would love to wind people up and laugh at their experiences.

One story that comes to mind happened in 1972. During the miners' strike Peter and his friends spent time in the local working men's club lighting their cigarettes with burnt five-pound notes. As you can imagine this kind of activity caused bad feeling among the members, who were finding it hard to make ends meet. But Peter knew the notes were worthless, because when he had blown the safe he had used too much Semtex, which burnt the stash of money. So he decided to pretend he was rich in front of the poorest people in the village. That trick went down with the members like a lead brick in a pond.

As time went on I grew to look up to Peter. He was a rogue but presented himself as a gentleman. When he and his wife Christine went out over the weekend, he looked stunning. He would have on his blazer and expensive trousers with crocodile shoes, and dripping in gold. Christine would dress in expensive clothes and shoes like the Queen. She looked amazing.

When they spotted me and my wife Paula in the local pub or club, they always made a beeline to speak to us. Peter would make us laugh and enjoy our day out. However he was diagnosed with Parkinson's, and from that moment on he started to lose his grip on life. By the end I hadn't seen Peter for approximately two years.

Then one day a friend told me that Peter and Christine had sold their house and moved to Spain. I was so pleased for them both, but my friend told me that they never got to Spain. I asked why and he said they had driven down to a port in the south to cross over to France, then drive down to Spain. But unfortunately the ferries had stopped sailing due to bad weather.

Peter insisted on cross the Channel, but Christine said 'we can't, Peter'. So in a rage Peter jumped into his car and drove away really fast. Soon after leaving Christine, he drove head on into another car, killing himself and the other driver. His actions were due to the medication he was taking for Parkinson's.

I never got to say goodbye or shake his hand, but I will always remember Peter as one of life's characters and a man who could light up a room with his presence. I'm sure he will once again make a beeline to speak to me when we next meet behind them pearly gates.

God love you Peter.

Also:

John Willie Graham, my father.

Eileen Rafter née White, my mother.

Trevor George Graham, my brother. I miss you.

Lou Harrison - your smile stays in my heart.

Ken Turner, my brother-in-law – great guy.

Bessie Tottey, my 'second mother'.

Wally Tottey, my great friend.

Auntie Glad, my adopted auntie.

Uncle Bill, a wonderful man.

Eric Hawkhead, a great guy.

Derrick Bean, a beautiful man.

Lillian Fawcett, a Welsh wonder.

Tom Westmoreland, a granddad in a million.

Dave Sharrat, a friend I will never forget.

Phil Tate, a man second to none.

Ian Slatter, school friend.

John Harper, school friend.

Dennis Allerton, friend, hero and my mate.

Paul Bull, a school friend who died aged 11 years.

Rita Jedinak, a school friend who was killed aged 12 years.

Neil Jones, a friend throughout.

Steve Railton, the son I never had and will always miss.

Norman Dwyer, family through and through.

Joe and Marjorie Leach, a wonderful couple.

Peter Crossland, a gentleman among men.

Charlie Scolland, Scottish and crazy, but a good friend.

Irene Scolland, Charlie's wife – the woman who put the flower in Scotland.

Russ Dixon, great guy.

Geoff Scuffam, a brother born to another mother.

Eileen Westmoreland/Dwyer, my mother-in-law.

Jack Westmoreland, father-in-law.

Gary Long, a baby – his death was too soon.

David Endersby, a friend in a million.

Bruce Teal, a joy to know.

Les Simms, a great friend and mate.

Printed in Great Britain
by Amazon

34796399R00096